SAVING YOUR SANITY
WITHOUT LOSING YOUR MIND

MAGGIE ANDERSON

ISBN: 1503107256
ISBN-13: 978-1503107250

This book is dedicated to Hank.

In our forty-seven years together he has crossed raging rivers, navigated stormy seas and beaten incredible odds all the while maintaining his common sense, practicality and good humor.

His is still the beacon I search for on life's foggiest nights.

ACKNOWLEDGEMENTS

Before I begin let me apologize to any pivotal people I mindlessly forget to mention. It does not mean you aren't important, it simply means I am not as young as I used to be and the gray matter is turning white faster than my hair.

I do owe a huge thank you to John Disposti without whose help this volume might have taken so long it would have to be published posthumously. From the bottom of my heart I thank you John.

My gratitude extends to my capable editors, Maggie Carr and Selenda Girardin, who took the raw materials and helped me smooth the edges and clean up my rusty spelling and shoddy punctuation.

I am indebted to Claire Robson who always believed I had it in me, to the memoir group that meets in Kendal at Hanover for their constant encouragement, and to the Vintage Voyagers in Haverhill, New Hampshire for allowing me to ramble every Wednesday and giving me a safe place to voice opinions and whisper fears.

Thanks to my friend and colleague, Charlie Glazer, for taking time from his busy life to say words of such kindness and flattery. My wish is to live up to them. Thanks so much Charlie.

To friends and family members who've read segments and offered insights and encouraging words you have my thanks as well.

MAGGIE ANDERSON

And to Hank and Aaron who maintain their good humor in the face of great odds; you give me the desire to do the same.

I sincerely thank you all.

FOREWORD

Commonplace wisdom is, oddly enough, remarkably uncommon. Everyone has opinions, everyone has advice, but not everyone has the keen sense of turning lemons into lemonade—with great good humor—that is demonstrated by Maggie Anderson in *Saving Your Sanity*.

From childhood memories of life on the family porch and her father's improbable encounter with the Hobo King through struggling with knitting and watercolors and learning to appreciate the simple things in life, Maggie will trigger your own precious memories. You will find yourself pulled into her world with glee. Remember that time when you started riding a bicycle and fell over and over again before getting it right? I do. Or when you started piano lessons and wondered how you could ever get both hands to work together? I do. Or the months that you and your spouse spent struggling to make ends meet yet discovered the joy of a (free) day at the beach, walk in the woods, or pillow fight? I do. Maybe you've experienced the terror and anxiety of a loved one's illness and have come away treasuring each day—each moment, each meal, each meaningful glance—in a new way.

Maggie has been there and back again, and she's here to tell you about it. She won't preach. She won't scold. She won't pretend to be better, smarter, or more talented than you. What she *will* do is help you to view your life with a fresh perspective and appreciate the blessings and obstacles that come your way. And she does it in deceptively short anecdotes, each of which still manages to create an entire world for you to inhabit. As a writer, I strive to capture the concision and color that Maggie offers, and I am in awe.

Every time I see or speak to Maggie, it's a breath of fresh air. She's funny, irreverent, and passionate about everything she does. That humor, irreverence and passion suffuse *Saving Your Sanity*. By the time you finish reading, you'll feel like you've known her for years, and you'll be glad you did.

Maggie takes incidents from her life, small and large, and uses them to illustrate how her indomitable spirit and her positive attitude have saved her from adversity. Perhaps they can save you, too. You only have to turn to any page to see for yourself.

Charlie Glazer is an award-winning writer (New England Press Association, Humor Column) and marketing professional. His weekly column, "News You Can't Use," has appeared in the Bradford, VT newspaper *Journal Opinion* since 1992. As editor of the *Journal Opinion* from 1992-1996, where he met and worked with Maggie Anderson, he wrote news stories, features, editorials and more. He has also freelanced for several publications and provided marketing services for Northern Stage, the Hartland JazzFest, and J.C. Manheimer & Co., among others.

SAVING YOUR SANITY

WITHOUT LOSING YOUR MIND

One Woman's Practical Guide To Butting Heads With The Universe

I'm sure you've heard one definition or another about what life is. Erma Bombeck, one of the funniest women who ever lived, jousted with the notion that life is a bowl of cherries. Life has been likened to a comedy and tragedy in turn. In the 1960's, life was a trip, sometimes a bad one but always a trip. I've heard it referred to as an adventure, a blessing, a miracle, and, on Broadway, as a cabaret.

As for me, I've always said that if I'd known what a difficult test life would be, I'd have taken better notes.

THE STORIES PORCHES TELL

Recording the porches of my childhood is a way of charting the course of my life. Some of my earliest memories are of Easter egg hunts, birthday parties and family gatherings at Uncle Lloyd and Auntie Florence's. They lived in a massive, Hacienda-style house in Duarte California. Its porch spread across the front of the house like a welcoming smile. My cousin Diane and I used to roller-skate on it. She had the only pair of skates, so, except for the times when we each had one and leaned on each other trying to stay upright despite our fits of giggles, we took turns, and on days when there were too many obstacles on her porch we ran down the street to skate on the big porch on the front of the post office building.

After Uncle Lloyd's funeral, family and friends gathered back at the house to reminisce and console one another. When I looked up from the front lawn I remember seeing all those people huddled together on that porch, and all I could think of was how they looked like baby teeth in the porch's broad smile, each with a story to tell of time spent there.

Before my sister, Eva, was born we lived in a trailer park Uncle Klein owned at the bottom of the hill from Uncle Lloyd's place. We actually had a patio, which in southern California is practically the same thing as a porch. My most vivid memory of it is intense pain. Dad was erecting a glider on the patio and I, not knowing it was supposed to be a surprise and my mother, not wanting me to spoil said surprise, ran a collision course. In an effort to see what was happening outside, I tried to push the door open, and

Mom was sitting on the step and she slammed the door shut. Unhappily for me, I'd already gotten not one foot in the door but two, and as a consequence I spent the rest of the summer watching all my toenails literally curl up and die.

Note: *Not all porch memories are fond ones.*

Gramma DeBow's patio was a haven and as close to heaven as I'm ever likely to get in this world. She always had a garden growing alongside her patio, and she watched over it with a furious zeal, her broom on the ready should a wandering cat try to take out any of the songbirds her little oasis attracted. She never actually whacked a cat; she just made lots of noise and waved her broom around in the air but the cats always scrambled to get out of her way.

The times we spent on Grandmother Fletcher's porch were as juicy as her pears, ripened to honey-sweetness in those Virginia summers so long ago. The visits when Auntie Agnes's kids were there too were some of the best times we had at Grandmother's. Mary Francis and Margaret Rose brought their hi-fi with them, and we cranked the volume up so loud the floor boards would quake. Sometimes we danced but mostly we just listened to the songs that millions of other kids on other porches all over America were listening to, songs like "Running Bear" with its tragic ending and old favorites with lines like "Put your sweet lips a little closer to the phone / Let's pretend that we're together all alone."

We and our cousins ate out there, shared secrets and stories out there, and plotted our life's strategies out there. Grandmother's big porch was our rumpus room, our deli and our executive office in one. Unfortunately for some, it was also our jail, the place of disgrace where my brothers and our cousin Michael were sent for detention after they stripped Grandmother's pear tree too early one summer. I don't know which was worse for them, the humiliation of their confinement on a beautiful and beckoning summer day or the terrible case of the "Georgia two-step," as Uncle Tommy referred to their affliction. Unripe pears were not meant to be devoured by the truckload .

Note: *See previous note.*

When we moved into the big farmhouse in Brookfield, New Hampshire, it was love at first sight for me. Not only did the house have a porch that seemed to wrap its arms all the way around the front and side, but the porch was veiled in purple lilacs. Lilacs grow all around my house now, and every spring when they begin to wake and in late May and early June when they bloom, I am transported back to the farmhouse. When I get nostalgic for the old place, I jump in the car and make a run for it. Some of my cousins still live there, though I'm sad to relate that the porch has long since been removed to allow more light to reach the house's interior, and the lilacs were cut down to make way for a bigger lawn.

In all fairness, my cousins did build a beautiful porch at the back of the house after the ancient barn was demolished. The memories there still float on the summer breezes; they're just not perfumed by lilacs anymore.

THE MEDICINE OF TRAVEL

Not long ago, my husband, Hank, and I returned from a harrowing journey, one that started out happily enough: a trip south to attend a miniatures convention and to see our youngest daughter and meet her new husband and the newest addition to our gaggle of grandchildren.

The air in North Carolina was brutal. Its effect on Hank oppressive and, ultimately, life threatening. He ended up in the hospital wrestling with pneumonia for the rights to the rest of his life.

So many things go through your head when you stand vigil beside a loved one in that kind of peril. To say it was a roller-coaster ride is the understatement of eons; no one has yet built a roller coaster that delivers that kind of knuckle-busting fear.

When we finally got home, Hank got some advice from a neighbor. He was told the best thing he could do from now on is to stay home and never travel anywhere again.

Our neighbor's advice, well-intentioned as it was, did not factor in the realities of the statistical data covering home-gown deaths and disasters. People die every day in their own homes. The accident rates at home are off the charts, partly because we spend so much time at home, but also because there are so many opportunities for breaking a leg, or your neck, so many opportunities to be electrocuted or sever a limb when an unruly chainsaw encounters an immovable tree trunk, and so on.

Television bombards us with so many advertisements for medical alert systems, their slogans have become punch lines for every comic from Vegas to the Pocanos. "I've fallen and I can't get up" has offered more laughs than its creators intended when they penned that line.

The truth is, no matter where you are in the world, your life is in jeopardy. If the air quality in China doesn't do you in when you're finally setting foot on the Great Wall, bird flu could pound you into mush before you reach the airport for your return flight. And though the plane could actually go down and take everyone to an early appointment with their Maker, you don't have to board a plane or visit some exotic destination to find your life out on a limb. A mosquito could nail you while you're mowing the lawn and West Nile virus could claim yet another victim. A deer tick could go unnoticed for too long and drop you faster than he drops off after dining on your unprotected leg. Home owners routinely fall off ladders while painting the ceiling or zap themselves while fiddling with toasters they've "fixed." Safety at home is a myth.

For those of you who keep your feet firmly planted on solid ground because you believe flying is dangerous, consider this, I just read the latest statistics and found human beings have a one in eighty-four chance of being killed in an auto accident, and that 35,000 – yes that's thousand – die in traffic accidents on American roads *every year*. If there were that many airline fatalities each year, the airline industry would collapse overnight.

There is no place on earth where people are totally safe from death or disaster. Staying home for the rest of your life will not increase your longevity. In Hank's case, it might actually shorten his. When he's spent his life looking forward to the next trip, being denied the opportunity to go anywhere would be paramount to telling him there's nothing left to live for.

Besides, Hank's always happiest when he's got a plan, a vision of something beyond the horizon. It is what has kept him going all these years in sickness and in health. We haven't told our neighbor yet, but we're already surfing the web to catch the cheapest airfare to Portland, two of our dearest friends, Verdin and Peggy, have promised to meet us at the beach.

Upstreet, across the country, or around the world, all we need is an excuse to pack!

GIFTS FROM THE UNIVERSE

I try to convince myself that every delay, every cancellation is an invitation to meet someone new. Being forced to stay where you don't want to be, or go where you hadn't planned, is often the way the Universe gets your attention; it's sometimes how you meet the most interesting people you've ever known. It can also be the only reality check you get for months at a time.

I met a lady in Nashville once while I was waiting for a plane that was delayed. I was crocheting, working on pieces I had to finish for a teddy bear show I was heading to. I had my scissors and my spools of thread laid out on the seat beside me, and each time I finished a piece I put it onto the pile of tiny body parts for that particular bear. I didn't usually finish the bears at the airport; I just made random pieces to be assembled later in my hotel room.

I noticed a woman sitting across from me, watching me intently. After an hour or more she got up and came over to sit beside me. She asked me what I was doing, and after telling her and sharing a snapshot of some of the finished bears, I asked her if she was coming or going.

She was silent for a long time, then she drew in a deep breath and told me her story. She said she had been at the airport since early that morning. She had five grown children who were all arriving that day, on separate flights from different parts of the country, coming home to celebrate their father's sixtieth birthday. She paused again, drew another breath, and said, " I've been sitting here all day trying to decide how to tell my children the doctor just gave their father six weeks to live."

Gramma DeBow always said the best way to stop feeling sorry for yourself is to look around you. She said no matter how wretched I might think my life was at any given moment, if I opened my eyes I would see folks who were worse off and had much bigger problems. Her theory was that if I spent time listening to and trying to ease the next guy's suffering, my own problems would shrink to a more reasonable, more manageable size.

The lady in Nashville proved Gramma was right. Had

my original flight been on time, I would never have met her. That single conversation made my life seem like Disneyland by comparison.

MAKING CONNECTIONS

Human beings cannot thrive without personal interaction with other human beings, any more than life can survive in a vacuum. People really do need people; personal connections keep the fabric of life from unraveling.

By connections, I don't mean taking up golf because a guy who could line my pockets tees off at three every afternoon. Unless we've already met and found we enjoyed each other's company, golfing together would be more avarice than friendliness on my part. The connections I'm referring to are those that enrich my life not simply fill my pockets.

When I was a girl we spent a lot of time in Laguna Beach, California. There was an old man who walked the beach or wandered around town visiting with folks, waving to people passing by in cars, and stopping to chat with those who gave him a minute of their precious vacation time. He was always referred to as "the old man of Laguna."

He was filled with information on local galleries and his favorite eateries; he knew the tide tables and the best tide pools and all sorts of trivia about Laguna's history and the surrounding area. I found the stories about him endlessly fascinating. The locals saw him as a beach bum, and in those days, in southern

California, beach bums were as common as seagulls. Yet when this guy died, he left behind a boatload of cash to benefit his beloved Laguna Beach.

As the old man's story illustrates, there can be unseen benefits when we make personal connections but those connections have to be personal first; the rest is gravy, simply a byproduct of connecting with the hen.

The first year we lived in Oregon, Dad came home and told us an interesting story about one of his connections.

Seems he stopped at Cubby's Restaurant, in Medford, for his favorite anytime treat, coffee and a slice of pie a` la mode. While he was savoring his treat, a guy wandered in off the street. He was a bit scruffy looking, and could have used a shave, but he was reserved and polite when he walked up and spoke with the waitress.

Dad said the man told her he had just come into town, and hadn't had a thing to eat all day. He offered to sweep up, clear the parking lot of debris or run the dishwasher for a while. He said he was willing to do whatever job needed doing, if it would buy him a bowl of soup or a sandwich.

The waitress told him she'd have to check with her manager, that it wasn't her decision to make. When the manager appeared, he told the guy that if he had no money and could not afford to pay for what he ordered he would have to leave. With that the manager started pushing the man toward the front door.

Dad jumped up to intercept the guy's heave-ho, telling the manager he would be happy to buy the man some soup and a sandwich and that he'd also spring for a cup of coffee and a slice of pie to top it off. Dad said the manager looked like he'd just had a shot of novocaine.

Before Dad and his new buddy got back to the counter, the waitress reappeared, coat and purse in hand, and informed the manager that she did not care to work in a place where the management would treat people so shamefully. Furthermore, she intended to split the guy's bill with my dad.

With the impact of a drum roll, the evening news came on and led with a story about that year's Hobo King being presented with the keys to the city by none other than the mayor himself.

My father always warned us about not letting our first impressions of people impress us too much. He said we might never know who we were dealing with if we didn't give the introductions time to mellow and fill out.

I guess you know who that year's Hobo King turned out to be. When Dad's lunch companion opened his battered coat and flashed its lining for the cameras, he had pictures of himself with dignitaries and politicians of all parties and persuasions tucked into those deep pockets. He had the keys to every major city he had traveled through that year, and shots of himself dining in governor's mansions all over this country.

What would Dad and that waitress have missed if

they'd let the manager throw the guy out? The Bible talks about entertaining angels unaware. I like to think one or two of my unexpected meetings were more than just a fluke. Perhaps the Hobo King was an angel sent to test Dad's level of compassion.

Sometimes the connections we make are fleeting, but their impact is felt from that moment on. I am reminded of an evening in Japan when I was sitting on the rock wall in front of my hotel in Yanaka, a tiny suburb of Tokyo.

It was an evening like any other until I looked up and saw a tiny Japanese woman, not a day under ninety years old, waving to me, trying to get my attention. As soon as I noticed her she motioned me over to where she was standing. When I reached her side, she pointed upwards, and there, hanging between the houses on either side of a miniature thoroughfare, was the most magnificent full moon I'd ever seen. It was magical.

Though it was just the moon, a moon that has risen and set for untold eons, that tiny Japanese grandmother didn't want me to miss it.

I have not gazed at a full moon since without remembering that woman, her sweet face, and her simple act of kindness, I doubt I ever will.

MAKING STUFF UP

I listen to conversations in elevators, at the airport, in restaurants; I make mental notes about clipped bits of conversations as I pass people in the street. Listening gives me a broader view of what makes the world spin every day, and offers endless story lines to write about.

Dad and I devised a way to improve our pursuit of new material for stories. We used to head for the airport, grab a cup of coffee, find a gate, and make up stories about what people were up to, where they were from, where they were going, and who they were meeting and why. We created stories of intrigue and suspense, having absolutely no idea who the people were or what their lives were like. But the activity gave us endless hours of free entertainment, and it honed my skills of observation as well. We didn't limit ourselves to the airport either; we zoomed in on folks in diners, in the lodge atop Mount Ashland, at the mall, even people just walking down the street - everybody was a target.

One night Dad was working on a story about a couple who were dining at a table across from us. We were at Kim's Chinese restaurant, in Medford, Oregon. Early on, this couple seemed to be just like any of the other diners at any other table in the place. But as time went on, their conversation got progressively louder until the pair of them were animated to the max. About the time the guy looked really steamed, and right in the middle of creating the back story for their little bubble, Dad gave me a nod and told me things were about to get interesting. Whatever disagreement they were having, was settled when the woman dumped a platter of spaghetti over the guy's head, and then stormed out of the restaurant.

When a waiter rushed in with a towel, the guy was just sitting there, his arms in a semi-lotus position, spaghetti and meatballs streaming down his face. Dad and I laughed so hard we nearly passed out. I can't even pass a Chinese restaurant without remembering the expression on the poor guy's face. Whatever the real story was, I wish I'd gotten it down on paper. I'd bet even money it would have been front page news.

THIS IS IT

John Lennon said life is what happens while you're busy making other plans. Why is it so hard for people to believe not only is this day, this moment, the most important moment in our lives, but it is also the only one we have for certain? Why do we let life pass us by while we are looking so far into the future we need a telescope? Why is right now not enough?

When I was twenty-six years old and Hank was twenty-eight, he had his right lung removed. We were sent home from the hospital with the admonition that we should "get our affairs in order." The doctors told us Hank would likely not see thirty and that we needed to prepare for that eventuality.

We had four children by then, all under the age of seven, four babies depending on us to get this right. Hank had no plans for an early checkout, but we were young, not stupid. When we got back to our hometown, we found a lawyer, had our wills drawn up, made arrangements for the house and the children, in case by some twist we both died at the same time. Then we packed a picnic lunch and took the kids to the river. After we polished off our lunch, we turned them loose to play on the riverbank, then we sat down and said, "Okay, this is it. This is all we have for certain, this day, this moment. Let's not mess around and waste it."

I am happy to say that Hank is still here, perhaps not moving with his former alacrity, but he's here just the same. We have never had two dimes to rub together, but we have always found a way to savor the moment. I hope we have shown our children the importance of every second, not just the times we imagine in the distance.

All too often that image on the far horizon turns out to be a mirage, and when we reach it, we find the things we passed on the way to "something better" were the things that truly mattered. Problem is, we can never get them back. Life is not a rehearsal.

THE DIFFERENCE BETWEEN
FRIENDLINESS AND FRIENDSHIP

Modern life makes it easy to let go of old friends. We find ourselves so entwined in the new place or some new involvement, we have little if any time for the old life and the friends we left behind. Connecting with new people and settling in to the new routine takes so much out of us that we run out of steam before the foam in our latte can go flat, and we realize we haven't spoken to our old friends since we padlocked the rented U-Haul and hit the road.

The people we encounter in the new location provide an abundance of friendliness. Friendliness is the server with the bright smile who dusts extra chocolate sprinkles on your mocha in hopes of finding extra cash in her tip jar. Friendliness is the hairdresser who politely listens to the woes of your week. Her sincerity is real, but it isn't real deep. She doesn't miss you enough to drop by with a pot of soup on the off chance you might be down with the flu; in fact, she won't have any contact with you at all until you call for your next appointment.

The checkout clerk at the new supermarket may well alert you to the fact that the item you only bought one of is on sale, two for one, that's friendly and helpful, but, unless you're wearing a name tag when you shop, he never knows your name. And the toll taker on the interstate may bid you good day, but believe me, unless he's your cousin, if you change your route to work, he won't even know you're gone.

Friendliness is pleasant. We need cordial interactions and bubbly conversations life would be grim without them but extra chocolate sprinkles are not what make a friend.

True friends will let you lean on them; they'll help carry your load. Real friends often show up with a pot of soup, whether they've heard you're down with the flu or not. Friends will listen to you complain about your problems with parents, boyfriends, kids, spouses or life in general. But a true friend also yanks the afghan off your lap and coaxes you outside for a day in the sunshine when they feel you've been floating on the couch in a sea of self-pity for too long.

Nothing snaps me into the now like the voice of an old friend telling me to get over myself.

A true friend is the first to tell you how bright you are, the first to brag about your talents, the first to defend you when you're right, but also at the head of the line when it's time to tell you you're way out of line. A true friendship lasts a lifetime, if it's tended to. Your real friends are behind you when life shines a spotlight down on you, and they're the ones waiting to catch you when you fall.

I have such a friend, several, in fact. Friends who have been there when I needed support, some who have pulled all-nighters with me; desperately guzzling coffee while trying to be ready for a show that was to open the next morning. My first boyfriend, who lived across the street from me when I was ten years old, still calls me on my birthday. I have a tight circle of precious friends who would be on the next plane if I called them in the middle of the night. Linda's one of them. She has often told me not to be so full of myself, but she's also always there for me when I need her. We've been friends for fifty-five years now. I barely remember life before Linda.

Linda has the build of a thirteen-year-old gymnast with golden eyes that look exactly like fried marbles and yellow hair that grows faster than the dandelions on my lawn. I always envied her that hair. And even after all these years, she still sounds like a third grader when she giggles or answers the telephone.

Like my aunt Vivian, memory is a bit peculiar, never responding the way we expect it to, sometimes not even the way we want it to. Don't believe me? Quick, think about all your birthday parties. See, the one you remember is when you were five years old and you threw a screamer in the midst of the celebrations because *everybody* got a present and it was *your* birthday! Or when you turned sixteen and your aunt Judy gave you a present filled with a rainbow selection of garments from Frederick's of Hollywood because she knew your brand new boyfriend would be sitting right beside you when you ripped that sucker open!

Memory has its own agenda. Once in a while a moment begins to wail with the intensity of a hungry infant who won't let up until it has been fed. That moment is the one I chose to share with you.

When I lived in Oregon, before I was married, every Thanksgiving our preacher and his wife would take the youth group to the beach for a four-day weekend. Any parents who wished to spend four days maintaining some level of propriety in the face of great odds went as well. Dad never went with us; the silence of a house devoid of six kids for four days was too appealing to him.

We stayed in a cabin in Brookings, Oregon. The cabin was owned by an elderly couple who had been church members since our church's cornerstone was laid. Their cabin was huge with several rooms for our gate-keepers and two large bunk rooms for the boys and the girls, one on the left and the other on the right. There was a massive open area in the center for dining, reading, or playing games when the weather was threatening.

If a place is big enough to accommodate twenty or thirty people and has lights and plumbing for a kitchen, one would reasonably expect bathing facilities. What we had was a little house out back with more ways for the Pacific breezes to enter than the half moon cut out of its door. A trip out there was exhilarating, to say the least. The little house provided a place of quiet contemplation, if you were quick about it, but that still left us without a place to take a bath.

The Pacific waters in the northern part of California and the southern part of the Oregon coast are so frigid, hypothermia sets in with the velocity of a teenager's growth spurts. The coast guard constantly patrols the beaches, on the ready to pluck out some hapless tourist who paid no attention whatsoever to the gigantic signs on the sand, peppered at fifty yard intervals from San Francisco to Portland, warning about the dangers of hypothermia.

In November, however, magic happens in that part of the Pacific. The thermal currents flow over from Japan and up the western seaboard to warm the waters, so we could swim, I mean really swim. We'd pack picnic baskets and hit the beach at low tide, scramble over the rocks and into the tide pools garnering treasures until the tide rolled back in. Then we'd chuck our blue jeans and t-shirts to reveal our swimmies underneath and swim until we got hungry enough to risk removing all the enamel from our teeth by eating peanut butter sandwiches and fruit salad, seasoned with sand.

By the time we started getting hungry again and our

inner thighs began to chafe from the drying salt and too much volleyball, we'd gather all the gear and drive down the coastline to California for a shower.

The campground at Ship Ashore, in Crescent City, California, had a bathhouse set up like a dorm bathroom, a row of sinks on one side of a long room with a mirror for each sink, and a row of shower stalls and changing rooms on the other side.

One night I emerged from my dressing room at the bathhouse only to find Linda standing totally naked, all eighty-five pounds of her, soaking wet, yanking paper towels out of the dispenser, right hand after left as though she were milking a cow. She'd forgotten to pack a towel.

I started to laugh, Linda began to giggle, and just as the other four girls popped their heads out to see what was happening, one of the paying guests entered, staggered, reached for a sink to steady herself, gasped, "Well, I never," spun round, and promptly disappeared.

There was a cartoon instant of suspended animation and then the six of us lost it completely. I laughed so hard I couldn't get a breath; I nearly passed out. The others were falling into one another, hanging onto their sides and laughing when Linda, still giggling, dove for an open dressing room.

We'd barely managed to wriggle the last pair of jeans over the last wet behind when the manager's emissary burst in to inform us it was time to leave, and would we please be thoughtful enough not to come back, ever.

I can still see poor Linda standing there, naked and dripping wet, with a fistful of paper towels in each hand, looking like a six-year-old caught in the act of trimming his baby sister's hair.

What would life be without friends like Linda?

MY COMFORT FOODS

When the pressure's on, very few rewards in life are greater for me, or more calming to my soul, than a bowl of steaming oatmeal doused with brown sugar and cream, especially if it's accompanied by a slice of home made bread, toasted to crispiness, liberally buttered, and submerged at the bottom of a mug of hot chocolate.

When humans beings need security, we run back to the places we felt safe in, back to the warmest place we knew. When storms threaten, we head for that happy place, though sometimes we have to recreate it in our own kitchens. My happy place was sitting at Gramma's tiny table with a bowl of oatmeal, its sugar-scented steam wafting up and a mug of hot cocoa warming my hands and promising gold when I got to the bottom.

There are many reasons for this, lots of science behind the calming effect of warm milk and good chocolate. For me, none of that even registers. The simple truth is, when life crowds in on me, squeezes me too much or backs me into a corner, I run home to Gramma's. Oatmeal and hot cocoa were her remedy for any despair she could not kiss away.

When Hank and I were dating, our favorite stop on our way out of town to the beach was Blind George's News Stand, in Grants Pass, Oregon. Blind George's made the best popcorn I'd ever tasted, and for a nickel we could take a sack of it along with us to munch on as we traveled the highway that meandered beneath the giant redwoods and followed the crystalline waters of the Smith River clear to the Pacific coast. Sometimes we just stopped for a bag when we were heading to Jack's Drive-in, where we always ordered a lemon or cherry Coke, Blind George's popcorn was the perfect accompaniment.

Blind George's is still operating, still popping corn too; in fact they pipe that aroma out into the street. I'm not sure how many fender benders it may have caused by now, so many drivers getting a whiff of that buttery goodness and hittin' their brakes to stop for a bag.

Even after all these years, the scent of corn popping takes me back to when we were young, living in the little house on Savage Street, when the most delectable snack we knew could be bought for a nickel.

Over the years certain foods have become my touchstones. The mere mention of them can transport me to other places, other times. The New Year's Eve dinners we've shared in our favorite restaurants, the buffet atop San Francisco's Fairmont Hotel, where we went to see Sid Caesar and Imogene

Coca to celebrate a house we'd just sold. The memory of biscuits stuffed with a sweet basil omelet we devoured while dining alfresco at the top of the hill behind the mint farm, where the winds blew across all that aromatic green and swirled around us one summer afternoon long ago, still lingers. When I think back on that day the wind blows the same mint-infused breeze and the biscuits are soft and flaky even after so many years.

Camping trips when Dad and I crawled out of the tent before anybody else, kindled a fire in the pit, and ran down to the river to fish for trout for breakfast still hit me when I'm in the woods and that earthy smell of pine and undergrowth fills the air. When I was a girl Dad told me that some day when I was an old woman I would remember those mornings and the aroma of breakfast over an open fire coupled with the pungent smell of evergreen on the wind. He was right of course, all these foods take me to a happy place, a place shared with friends or loved ones, back to moments of triumph and times of pure joy.

Comfort food is as individual as the snacker. It's like romance, to each his own and for his own reasons. All I know for sure is that when real life roughs us up we can pacify ourselves if we curl up with a mug, a dish, or a bowl of whatever takes us "home."

NOTHING LIKE A GOOD BOOK

Few things calm me down faster than reading a good book. I love books, especially books whose pages other readers have marked by folding down a corner; books with notes in the margins, a guide for the next reader of passages not to be missed or opinions needing to be shared. Research says reading a book, *a real book*, has been shown to calm study subjects and lower their blood pressure faster than music or massage.

The science of bibliotherapy notes the benefits of allowing yourself to be moved by a story, touched by its characters. It suggests empathy and tolerance are enhanced just by immersing oneself in the pages of a good book. But it must be a real book, study subjects did not respond as quickly, or as positively, to stories read on electronic tablets or from computer screens.

Three of my all-time favorite books, compelling stories of life carefully examined, well loved, and keenly appreciated are "Angela's Ashes" written by Frank McCourt, Rick Bragg's "All Over But the Shoutin'" and "The Diving Bell and the Butterfly" by Jean-Dominique Bauby.

Those are three men I would love to sit across a table from any evening of the year. Sadly, two of them are gone now, but I am still hopeful of one day sitting across the table from Mr. Bragg and sharing a conversation.

I find it impossible to read any of these books and still feel sorry for myself, still view my world as darker than anyone else's. I cannot read these books and still be down in the dumps.

PATIENCE : VIRTUE WITH BENEFITS

Much can be said about being willing to wait, especially for something you really love. Many of my favorite indulgences are specific brands or goods created by one person or available only from a single source. I could fold and settle for what I feel is second best, but, I can tell you, there's not a better coffee than my favorite, there's not a tastier peanut butter than my brand of choice, and there hasn't been a better cream puff since my father died.

Some things I'd just rather wait for. If that means going without coffee for a week because work and an otherwise erratic schedule make getting to my favorite coffee roaster's impossible, that first cup after a long, dry week is even better than I remember it. In that sense, absence really does make the heart grow fonder.

In a spirit of sharing and goodwill I offer a quasi-top ten list of my own favorite things.

COFFEE. The dark roast from Cafe Monte Alto, in Plymouth, New Hampshire, is so good I never leave home without it. When I travel, I order it roasted, ground to my specs, and bagged in time for me to pick it up on my way to the airport - that's how good it is.

PEANUT BUTTER. I love Teddie brand Super Chunky and not just because there's a teddy bear on the label. It is simply made with peanuts and salt or unsalted for the purest purists among us. It is unmolested, except that the peanuts are pounded to mush on their way to perfection. If you aren't a PB&J fan, never fear: Teddie is fabulous for sauces and unbelievable on a baked potato.

PERFUME. Shalimar - period.

CHOCOLATE. Whatever the brand, the darker the better.

MAYONNAISE. No matter how you spell it, BEST FOODS or HELLMANN'S, it's the only mayo that ever comes near my family favorite, crowd-pleasing fondue sauce. I wouldn't consider using anything else.

HAND CREAM. I am spoiled by the goat's milk lotion made at Wonder Fall Farm, in Franconia, New Hampshire. The owner makes a special blend for me, scented with Shalimar oil. If she hasn't time to get a batch done, or if I've run out sooner than I'd planned, her sage-scented one is the next best thing; it's blended with mint and it's earthy and mysterious.

CRAYONS. I never pay for crayons that don't whisper my name as I wander down aisles looking for art supplies. Crayola brand crayons are more than just crayons; they are a magic carpet I can hop on anytime I want to go home. And believe me, they do whisper my name as I pass.

TOOLS. I buy the best and take good care of them. When I started hanging wallpaper, Hank had just come home from the hospital following his lung removal surgery. I had four babies to feed, a house to pay for, and all the usual hassles everybody on the planet has to deal with. I had married while still in high school and had no formal training or higher education, but the kids still got hungry and the mortgage still had to be paid.

After a twenty-minute tutorial from Henry Burmiester, one of the best paperhangers in history, and one of the finest men who ever lived, I headed home to paper our downstairs bathroom, armed with Henry's encouragement that I had what it takes.

Henry told me to buy the best tools, that they would pay for themselves a hundred times over. I worked a solid week just to pay for those tools. I took very good care of them and am happy to report that Henry was right; I still have my original tools. If I needed to, I could wield them tomorrow and take care of any financial responsibilities.

A ROOM AT THE BEACH. I always get the room on the beach side, the one with the view I'll remember till I close my eyes for the last time. After all, you never know when you'll be back.

CREAM PUFFS. I swore off cream puffs after Dad died. His were exquisite - the shell buttery and crisp, the cream intoxicating. At least I swore off them after having tried them every time I got the chance for several years after we lost him. Then I decided I'd never find another cream puff as satisfying as Dad's. In the year 2000 I went to Japan for the first time and discovered a pastry company called Beard Papa's. It was a tiny little shop, squeezed onto a corner on the main drag in Ueno. I could smell the cream puffs before I found the sign. I just followed my nose to cream puffs so like Dad's I think the Japanese have found a way to bring him back. I look for him every time I'm in Japan, I haven't found him yet, but I always grab a cream puff whenever I pass that corner.

And for those of you who are fortunate enough to live in New York City, Beard Papa's has opened for business in the Big Apple. I'm praying for a reason to head for the city.

I PLAY WHENEVER I GET THE CHANCE

Play puts you in touch with parts of your brain that allow you to think, not only outside the box, but also outside your adult persona. I make time to play. The payback is immense.

I used to sell miniature teddy bears at a show in Deerfield Beach, Florida. Every afternoon the hotel would put on a huge barbecue by the outdoor pool. The moment those doors opened poolside, you could hear a giant sucking sound and every single collector would disappear for an hour and a half.

The show promoter was one step ahead of the barbecue though. She understood the power of play. She always stuffed our goodie bags with all sorts of interesting little toys, so for an hour and a half, all the dealers at the show turned into children, racing tiny cars, trying to set records with the paddle ball toys and tossing beanbags and sponge balls from one end of the showroom to the other. It was the most fun we had at any of the shows all year, simply because we got to play the whole time our customers were doctoring their burgers and salting their fries.

A BOX OF CRAYONS
CAN ALTER MY LANDSCAPE

Occasionally my family spent the summer at my maternal grandmother's house in the country, not far from Culpepper, Virginia. On the weekends we went into town to shop for the things Grandmother did not grow or make for herself. My brothers and cousins and I loved it when we were able to buy a new box of crayons. They were always Crayola brand. Even now, nearly sixty years later, that smell, that perfect blend of wax and pigment, is intoxicating to me. I've never been drunk on alcohol, but I have an inkling the effect of cracking open a brand-new box of Crayolas is as near to drunkenness as I could get.

I'm a great-grandmother now, and a new box of crayons is still one of the guilty pleasures I reach for when real life clouds my horizon. And even the biggest box available is still a lot cheaper than an hour on a therapist's couch.

At Grandmother's, my cousins, my brothers, and I spent countless hours decorating store-bought paper napkins with exotically colored flowers. Then the napkins were carefully folded so just the right part of the blossom showed when they were placed under the silverware as we set the table. Grandmother only used paper napkins when the gang was there. I think it was her one indulgence all summer, maybe Mom and Dad purchased them to save Grandmother some of the enormous effort of laundering and pressing the linen ones by hand.

Crayons, art supplies of any kind actually, ignite creativity; they refuse to sit idly by. A handful of crayons or a paintbox has the ability to transport me to the realm of my own choosing, and the trip always lets me hover above an otherwise mundane existence or less than perfect day. Art enables me to tangibly alter my view of the landscape and the tone of my own horizon. It lets me paint my own future in the colors I love best.

TEDDY BEARS AND OTHER COMFORTS

Reams of paper have been filled with notes on the teddy bear's impact on people of all ages. A special bear was created to deliver anesthesia to frightened children through a mask that was attached to the to bear's face. The dose was delivered when the child leaned in for a hug and a kiss. I know a woman who created "The Signing Bear" for hearing impaired children. The bear sits on the signer's lap, the bear's "arms" are sleeves which the signer's hands are slipped into. Then wearing gloves, that either match the bear's color or his personality, the signer talks with the children. Even the shiest of kids respond to the bear who's able to speak to them in sign. When my husband was in the hospital recovering from surgery, he was offered the use of a teddy designed to be clutched to his rib cage when he coughed. These bears are tightly stuffed, and intended to reduce the pain of the coughs necessary to ward off pneumonia. Their newest incarnation is dubbed "Sir Koff -A-Lot."

I have relied on bears of my own in moments of crisis. I have a bear named Ethan From [he's from Connecticut] who travels with me everywhere I go. He even has his own passport. I have squeezed him so often awaiting news from Hank's doctors about the results of his most recent tests, and long nights when I wasn't sure Hank was ever coming home again, that Ethan's passport now describes him as being scruffy-looking. I have even clung to him while undergoing x-rays and am happy to report the technician told me lots of other people show up with their bears in hand too.

I was once on a panel made up of teddy bear artists from all over the globe. The main question we were supposed to consider was the teddy bear's appeal to people of all ages and from all walks of life. As a panelist I thought the first question I should address was the question of why each person chose one bear over another. When talking to folks about their bears the number one answer to that question was then, and is still, "I liked his face."

That's straightforward enough and though there are variations of the answer such as, "he had a cute nose," or "a crooked nose," "he looked like he would be unhappy if I left him behind," the main allure seems to be the teddy bear's face. Everything else is less important, ie: his size or color, the outfit he's wearing, or not, even the feel of his fur.

The tougher questions are why do we hang onto our bears for a lifetime and why are they so important to us. My theory is a teddy bear becomes important to his owner because a bear is something we can truly and completely own. Think about that for a moment. How many other things in our lives do we cling to with the same fervor? How many things are truly our own? Not our clothes, surely, because eventually we outgrow them and whether we like it or not our mothers pass them down to a younger sibling or someone else's child. Likewise we outgrow baby furniture and bikes, even if we didn't a bicycle is often too big to be hauled across the country when the family has to move. I've never heard anyone say, "I had to leave my teddy bear behind because there wasn't enough room in the U-Haul."

Even our pets seem to disappear when the family has to find another home. If the new baby takes up so much of our mom's time she simply has to make a choice. The dog we've shared our secrets with or the cat we've cried on when life seemed unfair, is given away and we find ourselves adrift.

When we were children many of the things we loved were wrenched from our grasp by growth spurts, over-zealous cleaning sprees and the simple requirements of time or lack of space. Our teddy bears were rarely among the missing.

The reason teddy bear lovers cling so tenaciously to their bears is simple but profound. If you begin a relationship in an atmosphere of pure honesty and total commitment, sharing everything including secrets and sorrows, leaning on and responding to one another, you morph into a brand new entity.

My teddy bear is not only mine he's, well, me.

I am a member of the organization called Good Bears of the World. GBW was founded in 1969 "to ease loneliness and inspire love and compassion through an ageless symbol of love, the teddy bear". Since its beginning, GBW has given hundreds of thousands of teddy bears away. Bears are delivered to hospitals, and homeless shelters. GBW bears are donated to relief organizations following floods and other disasters. Hundreds of them were sent to the people displaced by that terrible nuclear accident in Fukushima, Japan. GBW members and clubs, referred to as Dens, have presented bears to their local police and fire departments in every state in America. The bears are wonderful for calming children in the face of fires and domestic disruptions. Good Bears of the World freely offers the solace only a teddy bear can bring to people all over the world.

If I find myself far from home, bearless and in need of something warm to cuddle, I know animal shelters and humane societies can use as many volunteers as they can find. There is always a need for help with feeding and walkies. And I'm sure I would not be turned away if I showed up with an offer to help at any shelter in the country. I could even find a warm furry cast-off friend there, if the cat who owns me would allow one in the house.

Studies have shown just stroking an animal can steady a person's blood pressure, reduce their heart rate and produce enough happy hormones to make them want to take all the strays they find home with them – well, maybe not all of them.

Then there's always the Hugging Bear Inn, in Chester,

Vermont. If Ethan's in surgery or had to be left at home I can adopt a bear for the night when I check in.

Note: My editor, who I fear may not have a teddy bear of her own, made the mistake of changing all the references to a bear, from he or him, to "it." I understand her point of view and I was willing to budge on the issue but Ethan wouldn't let me so all references about teddies are the generic, both sexes encompassing, he.

REKINDLING FLAMES

I was four years old and we had just been told by our kindergarten teacher that it was rest time. She never referred to it as nap time; otherwise she might never have gotten any of us settled. She drew the shades to darken the room and then she put Vivaldi's *Four Seasons* on the hi-fi.

The deal was, the student who was quietest during rest time got to go to lunch at the head of the line, holding the teacher's hand all the way to lunch and back. And don't think this was a trivial prize. This was our class's holy grail, a privilege most of us could never be still long enough to win.

I spread my blanket out, and the moment Vivaldi's first notes reached up through that hardwood floor, wrapped themselves around my heart, and connected with my four-year-old soul, I was mesmerized, paralyzed, could not have moved if I'd wanted to. I had never heard or felt anything like it before. When that sound shook those floorboards it became a part of me. I never wanted rest time to end.

When rest time did end, I took my place of honor and, holding the teacher's hand, walked down the hall to the lunch room. I kept looking back, not to see all my classmates bringing up the rear, but watching our classroom door receding and all the time wishing I could go back.

Hank and I have been married for forty-seven years now, and he can still flip my mood like a light switch if he puts Vivaldi on the stereo and throws a blanket on the floor.

Be it Vivaldi or the Beatles, music is a powerful force. Whenever I need respite from the moment, I reach back to the music I heard my grandmothers singing, or the silly songs Dad used to sing when he was trying cheer me up. And the songs that were popular when Hank and I were dating can remind me of the sparks that first ignited the flame that still burns between us.

Another of my favorite ways to calm down when life is a roar in my head is to put the coffee on and sit with Hank discussing some of the hurdles we've conquered and the victories we've won. It is soothing to look back and see where we were and know nothing can stop us when we're on a roll.

The other thing we love to do is reminisce about some of the silly stuff, like making love in the most unlikely places one could imagine, or nearly being caught in those unlikely places. Pass the cream and sugar and let the giggling begin.

Revisiting special moments or the silly episodes we managed to survive makes us more aware of the uniqueness of our lives, makes the moments more important because of that uniqueness. Each life is filled with wonder and surprise if we open ourselves to it.

WE NEVER LET THE LACK OF FUNDS KEEP

US FROM ENJOYING THE OUTDOORS

There is an Elysian spot above the water, at the trail head to Harris Beach on the Oregon coast. It is a perfect storm of elements. The wind whips through the salt-laden sea foam, skims over the waves, runs its fingers through the evergreen and the azaleas capturing their essence as it climbs the cliff side, then slams into your senses at the top of the ridge. There is not another place on Earth that sounds, smells and invigorates the way that spot does. The mighty Pacific offers up her treasures to anyone who stops by and never extracts a toll.

Crescent City, California is just down Highway 101 a few short miles from Harris Beach. When the kids were little, being flat broke most of the time created a need for truly cleansing breaths at an affordable price. Hank was sick so often we could never depend on a steady cash flow, but with four children to entertain we sometimes had to flee before all our heads exploded. Luckily, we drove a tiny Vega station wagon and five bucks' worth of gas would get us all the way to the Pacific coast and back.

We'd pile all the beach toys and buckets, blankets and books into the car and head for Crescent City. When we got there, we'd run to see the Colonel for a five-dollar bucket of chicken, drive down to the shore, spread out the blankets, feast awhile, then build a driftwood fire and turn the kids loose to tempt the sand crabs and stir up the tide pools. When everybody was sun weary and satisfied, we'd head for home.

In those days ten dollars gave us more for our money than any millionaire ever got for his.

THE DIFFERENCE BETWEEN BEING POOR
AND BEING BROKE

I asked my father a question when I was eleven years old, his answer has stayed with me all these years. He was sitting at the kitchen table filling out the paperwork for his property taxes. One of the lines was to be filled in with a description of the property. The answer Dad had written was something to the effect of "two acres and a shack." Assuming he was describing the house we were actually living in, I asked him if we were poor.

He told me being poor is mostly a person's attitude about money. If you see money as more important than it should be, if your feelings about your own worth revolve around the size of your paycheck or your bank account, you are poor, and if you don't find a way to alter your attitude, you'll always be poor no matter how much money you pile up.

Not having enough money to do all you need or want to do means you're broke. Broke is temporary; it can change in an instant.

After that conversation with Dad, I am here to tell you: I've been broke most of my life, but I've never been poor.

MR. TOAD'S WILD RIDE

I make jokes about having married for love instead of for money, but marrying for love has its benefits. The obvious ones are not having to sleep alone, having someone to debate with, and, most especially for me, having someone to bring me steaming coffee before I crawl out of bed to face the day.

I can see how having unlimited funds could be useful, but those funds could breed complacency; they could also limit possibilities. For instance, I have just finished getting all my travel ducks in a row for my upcoming trip to Japan. Had I unlimited funds at my fingertips I would have booked my tickets months ago, choosing perhaps a flight without layovers and I would certainly have chosen to travel during the most agreeable hours available. Cost would have been no object, so the things I might have missed would not have been an issue what you don't know you can't miss, and all that.

Fortunately for me, I learned a long time ago, the price you pay for something is not all it costs you.

When Hank and I were married we were, in Tevya's

words, " So happy we didn't know how miserable we were," so the lack of funds, though problematic at times, simply made us more creative. We found free ways to entertain ourselves, hiking or swimming, sometimes building a fire on the riverbank and fishing for trout to toss on the fire for an impromptu picnic. We used to drag a blanket down to the city park in the evening and just sit and watch the lights dancing on the ripples of the mighty Rogue.

When our first baby came along and we had even less money, our primary entertainment was often bundling the baby up and driving into town to spend an hour in the greeting card section of a local department store laughing ourselves silly.

After we purchased our first house and the other three children were born, Hank's health took a major nose-dive and I had to stretch every dollar tighter than most people can stretch a rubber band. Thank goodness I'd had so much practice by then.

Which brings me back to my current travel plans. I have purchased tickets that take me from Boston to Paris, where I stay for twelve hours, on to Helsinki for an overnight stay, where I have already reserved a room at, of all places, a Holiday Inn, and finally to Tokyo.

My return takes me from Tokyo to Helsinki, on to London, where I get to see the Queen's doll house at Windsor Castle, and finally back to Boston.

Some people would not see this itinerary as a plus, but in order to thrive on limited funds, you have to recognize a blessing when one appears. I have an opportunity, not only to see a doll house I've only read about and seen pictures of, but also get to add three more countries to the list of places I've been. I have the chance to sit at a sidewalk cafe in Paris and try a croissant in a place where they know how to make one. On my limited budget how else would I ever have found a way to do that?

The reason I booked this version of "Mr. Toad's Wild Ride" is because it was so much cheaper than any other flight going my way, and it left enough money in my kitty to pay for my bus fare to Boston, my train from the airport into Tokyo, my week's accommodation in Old Tokyo, my table fee at the Teddy Bear Convention, the overnights in Helsinki and London and the cost of most of the food I'll need while I'm away.

I would have missed so much in my life if I'd been in a secure enough financial position to write a check for anything I wanted. Many of my fondest memories are of things that happened because I was so broke I had to bushwhack my way through the money maze. I just may be the luckiest woman in the world simply because I have never had access to unlimited funds.

Being broke even saved my life once. Back in 2001, I was trying to find a flight to a miniatures show I was planning to attend in California. While searching for an affordable flight to Los Angeles, I found United's flight # 175 out of Boston's Logan airport. It was a bit pricey for me so I checked the flights out of Manchester, New Hampshire, hoping for a cheaper fare. After locating a flight leaving on the morning of the twelfth that fit my budget better, I booked the Manchester departure instead. At 9:03 AM., September 11, 2001, I stared in disbelief as United flight 175 crashed into the World Trade Center, killing everyone on board.

STICKING TO OUR OWN PRIORITIES

Hank and I have often been broke. His health issues have always been problematic for us. We had four children before his health spiraled totally out of control, and because he was unable to pull out of his health-related nose-dive, we had to work around it. Still, we never let our problems stop our momentum, we simply found another trail to blaze in order to reach the goals we set for ourselves.

For instance, we once bought a car too young to be considered an antique and too old to be considered desirable. Since we were dealing with an ever-changing cash flow we did not want a monthly car payment to worry about. I'm sure our neighbors would have found another car more acceptable but we wanted to take a trip to Germany and we knew we could not do both. We have our own priorities.

Believe me, over the years everybody we knew had plenty of opinions about what we should do with our money, even though we never asked them for advice. The truth no one warns you about is that peer pressure in high school is just a sample.

THINKING OUTSIDE THE BOX

When the kids were young, we decided to take them to Florida for a family vacation. We planned it to coincide with their winter breaks from school so that we would be able to spend Thanksgiving with my mother and stepfather. We planned to be away for six weeks. During that time I was planning to show my bears at a miniatures show and a teddy bear show, one show at the start of the six weeks and the other just before we headed home.

Since we never had much play money lying around, at least not enough to take six people from Oregon to Florida for six weeks, we had to find a way to raise some money for the trip. We told the children if they wanted to go, they'd have to help raise the money, and they'd have to pay their own airfare - no small job for the four of them.

At the beginning of the summer the six of us picked strawberries. Every morning we rose before daylight and headed to the field in order to pick in the early hours before the sun got so hot none of us could stand it. Then we'd head for a dip in the mighty Rogue River on our way home.

By the time the berry picking was coming to an end, the farmer and his wife asked us if we would help them with their garlic crop. We planted, weeded, seeded, picked, and dried the whole crop, working alongside the farmer and his wife and their kids. The day after we were paid, they took us all out to dinner and voiced their appreciation for our help, telling us they could not have done it without us.

Our kids had fists full of dollars, enough for their plane tickets and tons for whatever caught their eye on our trip. Hank and I had enough money for our airfare as well as money to rent a music studio and instruments for two hours of practice for the girls each day while we were there. The girls were all in the orchestra by then.

We did all the expected tourist stuff, ate regional specialties at every opportunity, and spent as much time as we were able in my favorite Florida town, St. Augustine. There we even found a great little place to get a killer breakfast by stopping a college student and asking him where his favorite place was. It turned out to be a huge breakfast, delicious and dirt cheap. We loved the fact that the place was teeming with all sorts of folks from all over town. College students always seem to know where to eat.

It was a trip we couldn't afford, but we found a way to make it happen. Dad told me even a dead fish can make it downstream, but if you want to fight the current, you have to be alive, kicking, and ready for a fight.

Whoever first said, "where there's a will, there's a way," must have been talking about us. We never let a lack of funds stop us from doing what we wanted to do.

OUR ALTERNATIVE RETIREMENT FUND

[ARF]

Now, more than ever, folks are cracking open portfolios, flipping through stocks and bonds, assessing their assets and toting up their losses. People facing the uncertainties of bleak unemployment stats and massive downsizing at heretofore rock solid American institutions are scrambling in an effort to keep pace with rapidly escalating living expenses and enormous mortgages; trying to put their children through college while still leaving them some semblance of an inheritance.

It is a mad scramble at best, fueled by fear. Not only are the foundations, laid down in happy anticipation of a comfortable future, rickety; many are crumbling altogether.

My portfolio is of a different breed. Amassed over more than half a century, it is an archaeologist's dream, beginning with childhood favorites clung to from one exodus to another, a few precious pieces of my grandmother's furniture, to things my family couldn't bear to part with when we moved across the country, and also consisting of the latest additions snagged for a song at local auction houses.

Many of those *treasures* we couldn't part with are now crammed into the nether regions of our attic. The original idea was to place them near enough so that we could go through them but not close enough to interfere with our settling in. We moved to this house in 1986.

When the last fledgling left the nest, we took over his room and filled ours with the contents accumulated for a shop we were forced to close after the owners sold the building it was in.

Things got a bit more crowded when we added stock from a booth I emptied because it proved to be logistically impossible to maintain. After that we had to evacuate antiques from a storage unit that flooded. We rescued what we could in the aftermath of the flood and brought it all home to be squeezed into an already half-filled cabin that was built for company. Let's just say it's been a stretch between guests.

Our woodshed is maxed out with supplies for our pool, the screened tent that keeps canary-sized mosquitoes from hauling us away once we leave the pool, and the first piece of furniture Hank and I bought for our first house. Any extra space in there is actually used for fuel to keep the home fires burning.

At the moment, I'm trying to find room for a load of bits and pieces from a booth I just closed in Vermont. When I take the stuff out of the car, I have no idea where it will fit. I fear that it may wind up on the porch along with all the other surprises hiding there.

The kids still have things gathering dust in the attic, though it's been twenty years since the last one left home, and there's no telling what long-lost relic could turn up in a serious dig of those first boxes we stored. One thing I know for sure is that if a tornado lifted this property aloft and set it down a hundred years hence, the story it would tell is the story of our lives, one room at a time.

Sometimes I have nightmares in which I see myself on an obscure reality show, the neighbors having branded me a hoarder. I assure you, I don't collect candy wrappers or roll used aluminum foil into balls, and the only cat in the house is very much alive, not to mention spoiled rotten. It is difficult to convince people you've just got a different sort of IRA. Mine's called an Alternative Retirement Fund, ARF for short.

If life throws us a curve and we need cash in a flash, I know I can do some digging and unearth a treasure I can turn into folding money. My portfolio is at the ready whenever I need it and is never affected by politics or the whims of the stock market.

Note: Whenever I hit my spell check button Hal (my uncooperative computer) politely suggests I try magpie, instead of Maggie. Last week I purchased a book called "MORE" featuring a magpie with some familiar propensities. The magpie collected so much stuff, she ended up not only buried under it all when the limb supporting her nest collapsed but was unable to right herself until all of her little forest friends came to her aid. I am beginning to think Hal knows more than I give him credit for.

LEARNING TO TRUST MYSELF

The year before he died, I interviewed the venerable Dr. Benjamin Spock. He was a tall and imposing figure with a warm and generous demeanor. One of the questions I asked him was what he thought was the biggest problem American parents faced at the time.

He told me that as far as he was concerned, American parents didn't have enough confidence in their ability to raise their own children. He said it bothered him that they were always reaching for a book or hunting for an expert to give them the answers. He couldn't understand why they didn't trust their own common sense.

My response was, "Well, I hate to be the one to point this out, doc, but you sorta' started that ball rolling." He told me he knew that, but he added that when he wrote his famous book on childcare, he stopped to tell me he just hated to hear it referred to as *The Baby Bible,* it was in direct response to the many parents who were calling, writing, or visiting his office with questions on childcare issues. He said there were no reference books available at the time that addressed all the issues he was hearing about in his practice. He said his work was meant to be a reference book not a Bible.

He was concerned that so many parents in the States were hunting for experts, that they relied on people who sometimes had nothing but their degrees and embossed lettering on fancy stationery to recommend them. He believed those parents would be better off following their own instincts and their own common sense rather than anything they read in books or speeches made by doctors and child psychologists, many of whom hadn't hugged a child in years.

I tried to lighten things up a bit by telling him my

mother-in-law had given me one of his books as a present when the first of our four children was born. I told him I had used it almost every day. I never actually read it, but it was so thick, it made a fantastic booster seat which all of my children had used.

We had a chuckle over that, and, I'm happy to say, he told me he wished more parents had done so, but it brought me full circle back to what Gramma DeBow used to say about psychology just being a hard way to spell common sense. She said we could all use a lot more of it.

One of the hardest jobs Hank and I had while raising our four children was standing our ground when other parents had opinions they freely offered about our choices for our children. As I've said many times real peer pressure doesn't begin until you have children; then everyone you meet tells you what you should be doing, whether you ask them or not.

We made choices with the best interests of our children in mind and, though in hindsight other choices may have delivered more positive outcomes, the choices we made were the result of trying to do the best we could for the four of them at the time. In the end doing what we think best for the people we love most is all we can do.

The truth is, there are no easy answers, and no sure ones; if there were the world would have no prisons and nobody on the planet would be afraid.

GETTING OVER MYSELF

Dad used to tell me not to bother sharing my problems with people. He said nine out of ten of them aren't interested, and the last guy's happy to hear I'm more miserable than he is.

I read an article this evening written by a life coach, a respected name in the business of helping folks reshape their lives and focus on what they really want to shoot for. She made some excellent points, I admit. She talked about the need to unburden oneself, to share what's bothering you and she gave some advice on getting the help you need to find the answers you're looking for. But come on: twenty-five paragraphs to say, "Get over yourself!" Good grief, how can anyone stretch that out for twenty-five paragraphs?

I cut to the chase, got over myself, and headed to the beach!

LEARNING NOT TO BE
SO HARD ON MYSELF

When I was in high school I struggled with watercolors. I practiced every free moment I found and still never painted a piece I thought was truly finished. Sometimes I did not like the way my background washes flowed; other times I simply detested my inability to put on paper what I saw in my head. I do not have a single watercolor painted while I was in school, though my art instructor asked if he might have one of my watercolors toward the end of my junior year just before I left school and married Hank. I remember how pleased I was that he'd asked for it but how puzzled I was that he wanted it.

Then an odd thing happened while at my big brother, John's, house for some family gathering or another. I found myself listening to praises about my watercolor skills. An old boyfriend, who is my sister in law's baby brother, was telling everybody how spectacular my watercolors were and how he always envied my ability.

I have been reminded of others' opinions of my watercolor skills more than once, each time I promise myself I'll back off a bit and not be so harsh a critic. My promise resurfaced one day at a teddy bear show. I saw the cutest little bear sitting on a high shelf. I supposed he had been placed there to give him more visibility. I asked the designer if I could look him over. He was a patchwork of wools, each piece perfectly juxtaposed next to a color or pattern that showed each off in its best light. The bear's nose was fashioned from an oval of beautiful, fawn-colored fabric and the embroidery on his face was exquisite. I had to have him, I liked him so much I was afraid to ask the price.

The designer wrapped him in tissue and placed him in a pretty bag, then said to me, "I can't believe you're buying him. I couldn't stand him. In fact I put him way up on the top shelf just to fill in a space, but I nearly left him home because I just didn't like the way he turned out!"

I guess I'm not the only harsh critic around.

CUTTING MYSELF SOME SLACK

We are truly our own harshest critics and, it's just possible, I am harshest of all. What people really need, what I need especially, is a reminder to be kinder to the person I am while aiming for perfection that I know will always be just beyond my reach.

While looking through a box of old photographs one day I came across one of me in a favorite purple silk blouse. I was startled by the image. I remembered how I'd stopped wearing that blouse because I thought I had put on so much weight it didn't look good on me any longer. I sat there staring at a picture of a beautiful young woman with a flawless body who, I imagine, was the only person on the planet at the time who couldn't see how good she looked.

Gramma told me you never want a glass of water until the well runs dry. I suppose that applies to the perfect body too. You don't know what you've got till you don't have it anymore.

Being kind to oneself takes practice for me, quite a bit of practice. But the older I get, the kinder I have become to myself. For instance, I used to make the same New Year's resolution every year. I resolved to answer all my Christmas mail by Valentine's Day, one year I nearly did. All those years when I didn't even come close, I beat myself up about it and spent some restless nights feeling guilty for not having found the time to answer the mountains of cards and letters from friends and family who had found time for me in the midst of the holiday chaos. The experience of self-loathing has been so bad, so debilitating I've resolved never to make another resolution the pressure's just too much, well, pressure.

SEPARATING MY "SELF" FROM MY JOB

Someone once introduced me as the Perfect Pear's dishwasher.

While it is true I washed dishes at a restaurant called the Perfect Pear, I am not a dishwasher. My early life was so bizarre, my husband told me if I ever write my memoirs I'll have to call it fiction because nobody will believe it was real. Yet I consider myself triumphant. I am victorious. I have survived that life and all its difficulties and retained my sense of humor and my balance in spite of it all. Besides all the jobs I've had to do over the years to make ends meet, I also design dolls and teddy bears, I write, and I have myriad interests and a lifetime of skills and experience in my back pocket.

I worked at the Perfect Pear because their need of someone to clean up and prep for the chefs, fit my need for part time hours in a place close to home. It was a job that allowed me to set my brain on auto-pilot in order to mentally design new bears or compose new lines as I kept pace with the stew pots and the seemingly endless mountains of potatoes to peel.

Washing dishes, or building high rises, or dumping

trash is what I do, not who I am. Too many people make the mistake of seeing themselves as their occupation, rather than as a person with varied interests and other plans.

There's a difference between a job and a calling. A job gives you the means to pay for the necessities of life, a calling allows you full expression, access to your true voice.

Remember, a job is what you do, not who you are.

NEVER BE DEFINED BY SOMEONE ELSE'S IDEA OF WHO YOU ARE

It is easy to be flattered by another's praise of you or your talents, but remember, it's just as easy to be demoralized by their disfavor. It's best to know yourself, your own strengths and weaknesses; otherwise everybody's opinion will mean more than it should.

I have a grandson who was born with a genetic disorder called spinal muscular atrophy. He has never been able to walk; in fact, he's not able to throw a baseball, swing a bat, or take part in any other sports kids of his age are engaged in.

He has defied the odds, has outlived most of the ominous predictions of his first few years, and although his life has limitations that are different from most of ours, he has found himself.

When he was two years old and still able to sit upright

unaided, one of his cousins was giving him a spin in an old pram I was selling at a flea market. As I watched them, one of the other vendors commented on how surprising it was that the little guy seemed so content just to be pushed around in that old pram. She couldn't understand why he didn't try to get out and run around.

She didn't know he couldn't walk, would never walk, would never do most of the things the rest of us take for granted, things like bathing or breathing, and these days even swallowing.

Aaron knew. He has always understood the things he can't do. He simply refuses to let even grim realities skew his focus. Aaron's focus has always been on now, what he's doing at this moment. What he can't do or may never get to do takes a backseat, behind what he's doing right now. He does what he is able, what his uncooperative muscles will allow. He's bright, artistic, and, most of all, optimistic. He will not be swayed by what others think of him or what they think he should or shouldn't be doing, we could all pull a page from Aaron's play book.

EVERYBODY HAS SOMETHING
TO TEACH US

Dad used to tell me you can learn something from every person you meet. Even my very own "wicked stepmother" had lessons to teach, though those lessons usually involved dodging tossed utensils and hurled abuses.

My stepmother was the ultimate dichotomy, meaner and more dangerous than a cornered badger but the most natural cook I've ever met. She could charm something magical out of any ingredients at hand. The aromas in her kitchen were absolute perfection, enticing and inviting. I'm pretty sure her culinary skills were how my father was sucked into the vortex of her chaotic life.

Even those who don't meet the highest standards of behavior can serve a purpose. My girlfriend Harriet's mother told her long ago that no one is totally worthless, she said you can always be used as a bad example. I guess my stepmother was proof of that.

SETTING THE BAR

During Hank's last pilgrimage to Dartmouth Medical Center, while on a mission to scrounge up something to eat, I passed a young woman who was knitting a baby blanket in an intricate pattern. She was using a beautiful mossy-green yarn and the blanket fell in sumptuous folds onto her lap. I stopped for a moment to ask about it. She told me it was to be a gift for a dear friend who had just given birth to her first child.

She was gone when I passed her little nook on my way back to Hank's room. I regretted not having taken the time to ask about her knitting skills. If I hadn't been so distracted, I would have asked her how old she was when she learned to knit, who her first instructor was, perhaps even found out what her first project had been and what she remembered about it. I let the moment slip through my fingers and now I'll never know.

As for myself, when I was seven years old, with the tenacity of a pit bull, week after week, I begged my Sunday school teacher to teach me to knit. Mrs. Ralston wore the most beautiful hand-knit sweaters and hats and gloves. She was constantly knitting baby blankets for the church nursery. At potlucks and quilting bees, while the other women set tables, served food, and shared their quilting skills, Mrs. Ralston was always at her knitting.

One magical Sunday morning before class began, Mrs. Ralston arrived with a ball of yarn and a pair of plastic knitting needles for me. The needles were the color and translucence of polished amber, they felt like glass in my hands. I was transfixed from the moment I laid eyes on them.

Mrs. Ralston told me to sit beside her and pay close attention. She told me to follow along and do exactly what she did. She began by showing me how to cast on, making sure I was careful not to pull my loops too tight. She tried to teach me how to snake my yarn through the fingers of my left hand as though I were practicing knots from a scouting handbook. She was a better teacher than I was a pupil and I am ashamed to admit even now I have not mastered that skill.

As I tried to keep pace with her, I fought my seven-year-old demons of inadequacy and prayed she was right when she said that if I practiced enough, I would soon be knitting like a pro.

By the time class began I had a few rows completed and was feeling a bit more confident in Mrs. Ralston's words of encouragement. I am happy to say I am still knitting, and anytime I'm tempted to give up on a pattern that seems about to defeat me, I hear Mrs. Ralston's voice in my head urging me on.

My grandmothers, my aunt Edith and others who've taken the time to teach me new skills and patiently stood by me when I faltered, are now the voices I hear in my head when I try to pass on the things I know. Each time a student masters a skill I've tried to help them with I hear the encouraging words of all those who stuck by me until I finally got it right.

DAMAGE CONTROL

The sorry truth about being human is that you will make mistakes, bruise egos, hurt feelings, and give offense often without even knowing it.

Sometimes the injured party roughs you up by telling you immediately they won't allow themselves to be so badly treated. I shout hooray for them, not only because it means they know their own importance in this complicated world but also because by speaking up they steer you to a problem you can attend to.

Other times you may blissfully breeze along not even knowing that you have hurt or embarrassed someone, perhaps even someone important to you. I am reminded of such an incident involving one of my oldest friends.

Carolyn was the first person I met at the new school when we moved to Oregon just before I entered the eighth grade. We were friends from day one. In fact, I can still hear that tiny voice yelling, " I will, I will," and that skinny little arm, surprisingly, even paler than my own, waving frantically for attention when Mrs. Morrie asked who would like to share their gym locker with the new girl from Utah.

Carolyn and I were more sisters than friends. Not only did we share a locker; we shared secrets, plans about a brilliant future. We even drooled over the same boy, which for us was where our first and only fight began and ended. I have six brothers, so I had a tendency to tease without a censor I'm happy to say I have learned to be more careful since the incident with Carolyn.

Because we both liked the same boy, we tried to get his attention every chance we got. He and I were walking together after lunch one day and Carolyn was following behind. She interjected something into our conversation. Without thinking I turned and said, "You know, if I wanted a puppy I'd have gone out and bought one."

I was so engrossed in the conversation I was enjoying with our mutual friend, I didn't even notice when Carolyn disappeared. I missed her on the bus ride home that afternoon and did not see her for a couple of days. When I called she was always busy or out. She simply dropped out of my life, and I, sensitive genius that I was, had no idea why.

I finally asked her older brother what was going on.

When he told me she was ticked about having been dismissed in so shabby and uncaring a fashion, I could not believe it. I didn't even know she was angry. When we finally talked it over, I asked her how long she had planned to avoid me and she said, if I hadn't talked to her brother, she might never have talked to me again.

Carolyn and I laugh over it now, fifty odd years later, but it scared me to know how fragile relationships are and how easily I could have lost one of the best buddies I ever had over some thoughtless remark. Happily for me, I am persistent and had no intention of not finding out why Carolyn was suddenly unavailable to me.

We still get a few laughs at poor Mrs. Morrie's expense too; like our reactions when she told a whole class of rapt eight graders that if we were in the showers and the fire alarm went off just to grab our towels and throw them over our heads. She told us with our heads covered we'd all look the same and nobody would know who was who.

We spent the rest of the day between wondering if she had finally snapped or who would actually follow her instructions if the fire alarm sounded. I'm telling you right now there was not a snowball's chance in the desert of my leaving the locker room with a towel wrapped around only my head.

SHIFTING SANDS

My earliest memories of my two grandmothers were

created in their kitchens.

My father's mother raised five boys and a girl alone in the midst of the depression, after my grandfather died when Dad, the youngest of the six, was two years old.

My mother's mother raised her two daughters and three sons, with my maternal grandfather's help, until he died when I was two years old.

To avoid any confusion, you should know we called my paternal grandmother Gramma, her last name was DeBow. But our mother's mother, with her southern sensibilities, was always addressed as Grandmother. At least this made things easier when one or the other cropped up in our conversations.

From Gramma DeBow I learned to wash my hands, corral my hair, and don an apron before I started any job in her kitchen. I learned to take just the slimmest of peels from the vegetables in order not to waste them. I learned to steam day-old bread in her blue spatter ware colander, to revive it so as not to waste any before the next loaf rose and filled her kitchen with that unmistakable aroma that always whispered home to me.

Gramma taught me to gather the scraps of dough after the pie crust was trimmed so we could make them into cinnamon pinwheels, which she baked alongside the pie. She taught me to save the cores and super thin peels from the apples she prepared for pie and showed me how to simmer them in a light syrup on the back of the stove so we didn't waste even the peels and all their sweet flavor. Many breakfast pancakes and bowls of oatmeal were sweetened with apple syrup made from the leavings of the night before.

My uncle Cal told me that when he was young Gramma always had a pot of soup warm and waiting on the old woodstove and that there was always a loaf of bread rising, or baking, or cooling, but bread always, should somebody come by in want of a meal.

He said evening meals usually included some bedraggled woman and a handful of children sitting at the table with the rest of the family. He said Gramma fed half the neighborhood at a time when she had an enormous burden of her own to carry, but Gramma couldn't ignore the women who could not feed their little ones. She figured that if she simmered a large enough pot of whatever she had on hand, there should be enough to share with those who were less fortunate and as far back as I can remember Gramma always managed to find folks less fortunate than she was.

The hobos who passed through town left messages for one another, saying Gramma was a fabulous cook but would not feed them unless they worked for their meal. When I was a girl, I asked Gramma why she fed the women and their children but made the hobos work. She told me she had no respect for a man who would take food from a widow with six children, and that he would soon have none for himself if she fed him for free.

I also learned how good liver was for a growing body, but, finding it the vilest taste and texture I'd ever had in my mouth, I balked at having to eat the stuff. Gramma would tell me I should be grateful for it because there were children in China starving for want of something to eat. I told her she was welcome to pack up my share and send it to them.

From Grandmother Fletcher I learned that nearly anything that grew on trees or in the field could be dried and revived later on, after the harvest was long past. From a gallon jug of dried-up, faded, unremarkable, sometimes unidentifiable bits Grandmother could turn a fistful of them into an ambrosial pudding or a batch of delectable hand pies.

One of my earliest memories of Grandmother's kitchen was the high shelf that ran clear around the room, filled with gallon jugs of dried fruit and vegetables. When my brothers and I were young Grandmother's reward for any job well done was a handful from the jar of our choice mine was always her pears.

Grandmother could scoop up a chicken from the yard, and by the time water was drawn from the well and the table was set, present a tureen of chicken and dumplings folks dream about, gravy to die for and dumplings so light you'd have to cover your bowl so they couldn't float away.

From Grandmother I learned the best dessert you'll ever taste is a dish of stewed tomatoes mixed with torn up bits of yesterday's bread and a liberal sprinkling of sugar.

These women taught me the value of conservation

long before it was in vogue. They showed me the importance of making do with whatever's on hand, finding a way to feed a family when there's no money to go to the store. They instilled in me not only a sense of gratitude for the things I have, but also an awareness of others and their needs.

When we got married, Hank and I did whatever jobs we had to to keep up with the needs of our growing family. In order to help feed my family, I relied on the lessons from my grandmothers, but I also worked at any job available, to make ends meet, just to put meat on my table.

Weeks when Hank was ill and couldn't get to work, I worked in the fields in the blazing sun for a dollar an hour because the grower paid at the end of the day and I could stop at the grocers for meager rations before I headed home. When we needed a new roof on our house and my husband's paycheck wouldn't cover it, I went to work part-time as a waitress – a job I loathed – and dismantled chimneys for a contractor on the weekends. I arranged my schedule around Hank's workweek so we had no need of a sitter.

In those early years we ate a lot of beans and potatoes. Many of our meals were not what we really had a yen for that day, but we ate what our budget allowed and what we planted and tended ourselves. Never once did we think someone else should work to pay for what we wanted to slap on the grill. I never considered leaning back and waiting to be fed or clothed and did not consider it someone else's job to care for my family. We took care of ourselves and looked after the needs of our own children.

As a consequence, our children were raised not to waste food. Our middle daughter was constantly appalled by the waste she saw when she worked in her school's cafeteria. She knew I worked for agencies that were always short of cash and whose outreach programs could have benefited from the trays of food being saved for the local hog farmer who picked them up each day the after the closing bell rang.

Her concern was not that the partially emptied pans were dumped after lunch but that trays of still untouched sandwiches or pizzas were trashed before ever facing the fluorescence of the serving counter. She petitioned the school to have the homeless shelter pick up the untouched food at the end of each day, but her plea was never heeded. That hog farmer had some of the best stock in the state, fed on some of the best food he ever slopped.

During our lifetime we have watched America's attitude shifting like sands in the desert, slowly suffocating the lessons we learned from our ancestors and burying forever their sense of independence and self-reliance. Those lessons have been swept off our mental maps by a pervading belief that we should have whatever we want, whenever we want it even if someone else is forced to pick up our tab.

Every time Hank and I go out to eat we see folks order food they do not finish but don't take home for later either. Children ask for items they decide they don't want. That food gets tossed by busboys that make minimum wage and probably can't afford to eat in the places where they work.

Hank and I celebrated our forty-sixth wedding anniversary by dining out. We chose a restaurant a friend recommended. She said the food there was wonderful and the ambiance conducive to conversation and a memorable evening. We dressed for dinner, me in an outfit set off by a favorite antique hat, he in his tux. We don't go out much so we thought we'd make the most of it.

Dressing for dinner must be as outdated as the adage waste not, want not, because there were more folks dressed in tank tops and flip-flops than in any restaurant I've ever patronized.

Americans are spoiled by abundance. We have forgotten what it is like not to have enough. When we can go anywhere we choose, order anything we desire, as often as we wish, nothing is special. "Dinner out" no longer has any significance.

Americans waste more food than the people in most countries eat. We simply have too much. Our abundance causes us to forget the feeling of want. It keeps us from seeing the plight of people all over the globe who struggle to feed themselves every single day. Having too much is worse than not having enough because not having enough means we have to think about the consequences of our actions, find ways to stretch our budgets. Most importantly, having too much keeps us from knowing how fortunate we are.

PENNIES FROM HEAVEN

I was checking out of a grocery store yesterday and noticed a penny on the floor near the register, I told the boy behind me that it must be his day because there was a lucky penny right at his feet. His smile was bigger than the penny's worth these days but it reminded me of what Dad used to do when I was a girl.

Whenever we came out of a store, if Dad still had change in his hand from his purchase, he tossed it onto the sidewalk. He loved to sit back and watch the reactions of the kids who would find it as they passed, he got the biggest kick out of the happiness a handful of change could give.

I found out part of the reason for his behavior when he told me a story about when he was a boy. My grandfather was killed when my dad was only two years old. He was the youngest of Gramma's six children, too young to help carry Gramma's load. His oldest brother became the man of the house and the other siblings stepped in to do what they could but Dad always felt as though he was part of his mother's burden.

He told me of the day he found a five dollar bill in a gutter and how he'd run all the way home with it crumpled up in his hand. I remember the joy on his face when he said he gave it to his mother and felt, for the first time, that even he could make a difference.

I cannot remember a time in my life when I wasn't

surrounded by amazing people, with amazing stories to tell, some triumphant, some troublesome in the best light, and others the stuff that made my life a kaleidoscope of brilliant bits that sparkle in the sunlight of my memory.

The story tellers in my family harken back to a time when ordinary accomplishment became legend and families built a reserve of pride, courage and stamina on the foundation of the stories they passed down. The stories of how my grandmothers beat seemingly insurmountable odds and lived long and productive lives in spite of those odds is the stuff my own resolve is built upon.

The family's history, told in bits and pieces, a moment here and a snapshot there, is better than pennies from Heaven. I can still see the sparkle in my father's eye when he told me about that crumpled five dollar bill.

CREATING MY OWN HAPPINESS

Statistically, America is ranked seventeenth on the list of the happiest countries in the world. Seventeenth! We've fallen from the lofty heights of number sixteen in 2004. Back then, the folks in Nigeria were counted as the happiest people on the planet! How can that be? We live in a country that residents of almost any other country in the world consider nothing short of the Holy Grail. We have not only a diverse landscape, some of the most breathtaking sights in the universe, but also freedoms in nearly every aspect of our lives that most of the people of the world envy.

I remind myself every day that happiness is a choice and one I should hang onto with vise grips. A wise man once wrote, "Happiness is an inside job." He was right. Human beings have the power to *be happy* if we choose to. It takes very little effort, and the rewards are huge. With a few simple tweaks in our behavior and our thinking, we could rise in the ranks to become the happiest people on earth.

As a child I simply told myself one sunny southern California morning in the midst of the family's usual chaos, I was going to be happy whatever came my way. Life has not always been easy on me I didn't expect it to be. But I was then, and am now, determined to be happy regardless of what happens in my Personal Universe, and, believe me, there are days when that's PU for short.

There are still times when I have to reach into the guts of a huge cloud, grab onto a handful and rip that sucker inside out just to find its silver lining. But I'm here to tell you it can be done. At Hank's recent eye examine I listened to the doctor's litany of Hank's problems from his possible need of laser surgery, to macular degeneration and ultimate blindness. Part of me wanted to scream about the outrageousness of his spending the first thirty-five years of our marriage battling lung problems, the next six or seven years dealing with a bum ticker and finally the prospect of losing his sight. I just felt like throwing the window open and screaming, "Can't the guy catch a break?" But I got hold of the inside of that cloud and reminded myself that the only fantasy I ever entertained was of making love to a blind man, if things don't work out well for Hank, I may just get that chance.

Modern science has taught us the truth of the old songs and sayings we heard our grandparents singing or espousing. Human beings have the unique capability of making themselves happy, literally creating their own happiness, just by raising the corners of their mouths. "Look on the sunny side of the street" is more than just a phrase set to a catchy tune; those words are a path to the happiness we're all in pursuit of. Trouble is most of us don't believe we create our own.

When we simply activate the muscles necessary to put a smile on our face we drench ourselves in so many happy hormones it is impossible for our brains to head us off at the pass. The act of smiling floods the brain with serotonin, nature's "feel-good" hormone, and laughter suppresses the brain's ability to produce stress hormones. It turns out we can fake it till we make it after all.

Just in case you're wondering if the reverse is true, I offer this. A psychologist from the University of Chieti-Pescara in Italy, Daniele Marzoli, Ph.D. says squinting makes us angry. People's emotions were tracked when the sun was either in their face or at their back. Squinters reported feeling 44 percent more agitated and aggressive. When we squint, we create what is essentially a frown that sends a signal to our brain that we're irritated, even if we weren't angry to begin with. Our mood is linked to our facial muscles. Whether we present a smile or a frown our brain takes over from there and for the rest of the day we pick up the tab, or the folks around us do. The worst part of Marzoli's findings is that irritation flares up almost instantly!

So when life drops another bundle of dirty laundry on my lap, I tip my head to the sun, put a smile on my face, and I am soon thanking Providence not only for the strength and skill to handle my bundle of laundry, but I'm also celebrating the fact that the sun came out just in time to dry the whole load.

SHARING THE BURDEN
SPREADING THE JOY

The year Hank had his lung removed, we'd been married for almost eight years and had four babies from two to seven years old. Our fourth baby was born before the first one turned five.

To say life was hectic and I was often stressed to the max would be like saying Mount Saint Helens burped in 1980. I knew I had to maintain some sort of peaceful personal center but had to find a way to achieve it without money or at least with very little of it.

I love to roller skate. There is something so freeing about just hitting the skating floor and letting the wind in my face strip my cares away. Our local rink had a seventy-five-cent coupon for a Tuesday night special. If you had a coupon from the week before, not only did you get to skate from seven to nine pm. but you also got a soft drink with the same coupon and another coupon to skate the following week.

My girlfriend Trish had three children and was usually as broke as I was, but when Tuesday rolled around, we found a way to skate no kids, just a big girls' night out. I hate to think how I would have coped had I not been able to get away on Tuesday nights.

In order to pay for skating I sometimes had to scrounge up pennies from the car's ashtray and delve under the couch cushions. Other times I hauled all the soda bottles I could find up to the grocery store for the redemption money. I knew I had to have a moment for myself so I could be strong enough to face another week.

Finances were so tight in those days, Trish and I would often run to the store on our way home, buy a loaf of bread and a gallon of milk to split, in order to fix breakfast for our kids the following morning. One of us always carried a plastic bag and an empty jug so we could divvy up the loot.

Being able to share our predicament made it more bearable for each of us. My load weighed half as much with someone else to help me carry it.

HEALING AND HUMOR
TWO SIDES OF THE SAME COIN

The night of my father's funeral the family gathered at my big brother, John's, house to visit, to reminisce. All of Dad's surviving brothers were there, along with their wives, and several of our many cousins. That night while listening to my father's brothers, my brothers and I learned things about Dad we'd never known. Our uncles shared stories we had never heard and I always said we found out more about our father the day we said goodbye to him than we'd ever known before.

Though it was a somber occasion when you get a gang of my family members together for any reason, the jokes begin to bounce off every person in the room, they fly like ping-pong balls, bringing a new one to mind as soon as the last one's laughter fades away, sometimes even before.

The problem for me that night was I chose to sit within arm's reach of my cousin Currie. Every time he sensed the coming punchline, he would reach out and slug me on my arm and, on the rare occasion he didn't guess it ahead of time, the punchline would cost me even more, as soon as he heard it he would slug me repeatedly as the tears just poured down his cheeks. Believe me, I shed some tears that night myself and it wasn't just because we'd lost Dad. And the laughter we shared helped to heal the gash my father's untimely death opened up.

DISNEYLAND BY ANY OTHER NAME

The summer before I entered the eighth grade we left Salt lake City, Utah and moved on to Dad's original, intended destination, the agate flats, in the shadow of majestic Mount Pitt in White City, Oregon. I lived on that property from eighth grade, through three years of high school until I met and married Hank at the end of my junior year.

My school friends lived a life so different from mine, we may as well have been on different planets. They lived in Disneyland, and the chasm between their universe and mine was immense.

Lots of my girlfriends sported the latest hairstyles. In contrast, if I wanted to wash my hair I had two choices. I could either prime the pump at the end of the drive and wash in the frigid, sulfuric stream or I could hike the half mile to the laundromat and hope that nobody was soaking their work clothes in the sink. If the sink was empty I actually got to wash my hair in warm water.

Of course in the summertime clean up was a no-brainer. Dad would tie a bar of Ivory soap up in a mesh onion bag, attach the end of the twine to a tree branch and we'd all take turns bathing in the mighty Rogue River. These were guilt free baths because the advertisements for Ivory soap always promised their product was 99.99% pure.

The popular girls walked the halls of school looking like the pages from a fashion magazine. I remember once refusing to go back to school until I got a new pair of sneakers from the eighty-eight-cent store. The cereal box Dad had cut and pasted into my shoes the week before had flopped out onto the floor of the main hall and I spent the rest of that day with the bottom of my feet in constant contact with the linoleum floors in order not to sound like a duck running to catch raindrops.

I had a hideous, puffy jacket, bright blue in color. I was four-foot-ten-inches tall at the time and when I wore that thing I looked like a giant blue beach ball rolling down the hall. My hatred for that jacket had even more to do with how it came to be mine than how I looked in it.

Dad had asked each of us what we really wanted for Christmas that year. What would we ask for if we could have virtually anything we wanted. I dreamed of owning one of the coats popular at the time. It was a coat of soft wool with a fur collar, granted, the fur was fake, but the illusion it produced was enchanting. I wanted one of those coats if only to feel a touch of class for a second and a half.

On Christmas morning I got the blue beach ball and the news that my stepmother had talked Dad out of the coat I wanted because, first, it was totally impractical and second, because it was simply too expensive anyway. My hatred for that jacket was trumped only by my resentment for what my step mother had done.

My freshman year, a classmate arrived at school one morning with eyes more emerald than the real gems. Her folks had sprung for colored contact lenses. For weeks she was the envy of nearly every girl who was forced to wear glasses. I was not among them, though I thought she looked fabulous, mysterious and intriguing, all I wanted was to be able to see what assignments were written on the blackboards without having to sit close enough to actually reach out and touch them.

I told my father I wasn't going back to school my sophomore year unless I had glasses before the school year started. By then I think Dad knew not to test me. I had refused to go back to school until I got those sneakers the year before. I'm sure he thought the mood would blow over, but soon grew tired of me sitting at the house all day for a week and finally relented and took me to the store for shoes. The funny thing was when the sales clerk came to see if we needed help Dad looked her square in the face and said " These women, they'd wear those stupid sneakers till they fell right off their feet if you'd let 'em."

My classmates were punished for infractions by having privileges revoked, or by suffering the injustice of being grounded for having missed curfew or flunking an algebra test. Some of the guys got a thumping for coming home drunk and being sick all over the brand new wall to wall carpeting.

My step mother's idea of punishment for me was a two-by-four to the side of my head. She was so bent on my destruction, I was relieved when the cement foundation we poured for the new house solidified into concrete. If she did me in, at least she'd have to find another place to dump my body.

An old tree farmer lived on the northern side of the flats from where we settled in to build Dad's dream house. If memory serves, the farmer's name was Olson. It was more than fifty years ago, I could be wrong, but for now, Mr. Olson he is. Though his name may be a bit foggy to me, I still remember the things he said about trees and life in general.

I was visiting one morning as he was closing a sale. After helping his customer load the chosen tree onto the bed of his pickup truck, Mr. Olson gave the guy a jelly jar filled with blue-colored liquid and instructed him to stir ten drops of it into a five-gallon bucket of water and pour it over his new tree every morning for the first month after transplanting it. Mr. Olson told him the drops were nutrients his tree needed and that it would suffer without them. [Turns out it was just colored water but Mr. Olson told me, stressing the importance of using the blue liquid was the only way he could be reasonably sure the customer would give the new tree all the water it needed for a solid start. Besides, he reminded me, there were plenty of nutrients in the water.]

Next Mr. Olson handed the guy a handful of reeds and told him to give his new tree a good smackin' around each morning: "Rough 'im up pretty good. Don't go too soft on 'im." The man asked Mr. Olson if he was serious, and Mr. Olson assured him that he was indeed.

He said, "A tree that's left to grow up spoiled don't grow up to be much, but if life [or presumably the new owner] gives it a smackin' once in a while, it will build up a strength that will help it survive whatever comes its way."

I'm not sure the guy believed him, but he took the reeds and left with his tree.

I asked Mr. Olson if he thought the guy would really give his tree a beatin' every morning, and he said, "Probably not. Folks are so afraid of pain or disappointment; they can't see it doin' any good. But ya' see, the strongest people are like the strongest trees: They've been roughed up some and tested; they're stronger for it, and they know they can take whatever comes."

If I assess my life according to Mr. Olson's standard, I should be the strongest woman in the world by now.

THE ART OF DODGE BALL

We all have friends or family members who know, beyond any doubt, that their problems are worse than anyone else's, who refuse to see anybody else as being in need or to acknowledge another's plight.

Naturally, these are also the people who are just as certain I'm the one with whom to share their woes.

The biggest problem with these folks is they don't take any of the advice I offer, nor do they come up with their own plan for escaping the mire of their misery. It seems they are not happy unless they are miserable, are not content until you, or I, finally after all their hysterics, see them as victims as well.

I'm not suggesting I write these unhappy campers off completely, many of them are family, after all. But I will say this, if I don't find a way to separate myself from their miseries, there is a distinct danger of their issues becoming my own.

"Misery loves company" is more than a saying our grandmothers repeated; it is a fact as true as the age printed on my driver's license. Misery is a silent enemy, creeping up on you without rippling the water. Like ice crystals, miseries gather strength and size below the surface. If I am not careful, before I know it, they'll become an iceberg capable of sinking my ship.

If, after honest and sincere effort on my part, these sad victims refuse to let me hose them down or cheer them up, my only course is to hug them warmly, wish them well and run like a frightened rabbit. Life is far too short to sit in one place and spin my tires.

Lately I've become more aware of how quickly my window on life is closing. I'm not planning to check out anytime soon, but I'm not getting any younger either. The fact that time is drawing a bead on me creates an acute awareness of how precious the time I've got left is. I cannot waste a second of it trying to rally those who don't want to be on the squad, those who would rather complain than see life from a brighter perspective.

I owe it to myself to make the most of every minute I have left.

Every school child knows when playing dodge ball, a moving target is hardest to hit. I remind myself that even the preflight instructions tell me to don my own oxygen mask first in order to help those around me.

BE CAREFUL!

YOUR SANITY IS NOT THE ONLY THING YOU HAVE TO LOSE

On my way home from work I pass through an intersection called Four Corners. I quickly scoot across, after checking and rechecking for traffic coming from either direction; the vehicles come instantly and seemingly out of nowhere there, not being alert could cost me everything.

A young woman named Tammy died at that very spot not so many years ago because her father miscalculated the speed and distance of a semi barreling down on them. The debris, spread from the intersection to the firehouse at the top of the hill, was scraped and swept into heaps by the side of the road like autumn leaves raked together and piled on the lawn.

Tammy had decided to ride home from college with her folks instead of her boyfriend because she said, " I just feel safer with Daddy at the wheel."

Every time I cross that intersection I am reminded of her and the sad fact that she never made it home for Christmas.

IDENTIFY YOUR PHOTOGRAPHS WHILE YOU OR SOMEBODY IN THE FAMILY CAN STILL RECALL WHO'S WHO

Last night I bought a box at an auction, a time

capsule of sorts, containing flotsam and jetsam collected over the past twenty-five years or so,including a calendar with daily entries signifying everything from dentist's visits to yoga classes,each month a thumbnail sketch of the owner's life. From the foreclosure papers in 1985 to an undeveloped roll of 35mm film and a stack of unidentified photographs, everything in the box has something to say. Sadly, the photographs could have shed more light on the box's owner if someone had taken the time to jot a date and a note on the back of each one.

The whole carton of the stuff of someone's life just screams to be written down as a testimony to the world that their life was valuable, not just to themselves but to each of us struggling in the same gray soup.

At a different auction several weeks ago I bid on another box and found a photo of a grown man wearing a broad grin and sitting next to Santa. Who knows who they were or what their connection was? If only someone had thought to write it down.

I have a photograph of Uncle Cal and his only sister, my aunt Ruth, identifying a bunch of my old family photographs at Portland International Airport as she and I waited to board a plane for home.

I still have a stack of photos filled with unnamed faces and faraway places that, sadly had not been identified for me before Uncle Cal and Auntie Ruth died. I have my work cut out; it will not be easy to find a name for so many faces. How I wish I had asked more questions while I had the chance and

Uncle Cal and Auntie Ruth still had the time.

MY COUSINS

I was flipping through memories this afternoon, recalling moments spent with some of my cousins. The space my cousins have occupied has always been a happy place. As far back as I can remember I was surrounded by cousins. My cousin Bethany's face is as constant in the reflections of my early years as my mother's. Bethany had a knack for making anyone she was with feel as if they were the most important person in her universe, no ordinary accomplishment.

Bethany must have learned this skill from Gramma DeBow, who had the same effect on me. Of course, I knew I really was her favorite. When I was first married I went home to retrieve the rest of my things from the house on Merry Lane only to find that Uncle Cal's little house, next door to ours, had been ransacked. The thugs had tossed everything out onto the ground and then scattered across the driveway anything they felt had no value.

As my new husband and I were scooping everything up I noticed Gramma's unmistakable handwriting on several letters. I opened one and burst into tears after reading the first line. It read: "Dear Leland: So tell me, how's my precious Peggy?" Until I was eight years old, I didn't know my name wasn't actually Peggy; everybody called me Peggy. I always believed Gramma loved me best, now I had proof!

Dad and Uncle Cal, whose real name was Leland, his

brothers gave him the Cal moniker because he was shy and as silent as president "Silent Cal" Coolidge, were the models for the Bobbsey Twins, so Uncle Cal's son Arthur was around from the beginning. Remembering scenes with Arthur in them can make any miserable day brighter.

There was one morning in California I can picture as though it was happening now. Arthur was about eighteen months old and he was playing on the patio. When Auntie Mona looked over at him she noticed he had a snail in his hand. He was just watching it slink around in its little shell and stick its tiny feelers out. But Auntie Mona yelled at him to "put that dirty thing down this instant" and poor Arthur, in a panic he was about to lose his new companion, took one last desperate look at Auntie Mona, and, before she could close the gap between them, he sucked that little thing out of its shell and swallowed it whole. I can still see the look on Auntie Mona's face. I don't know how she managed not to pass out. I laugh so hard I nearly pass out myself every time I think of it.

Memories of Arthur fill lots of pages in my mind's scrapbook.

As I got older, my cousins became even more important. Their companionship served as a buffer between me and a difficult existence. They shared their secrets and kept some of mine. They became my strength; they offered a glimpse of a life I did not know.

Uncle Lloyd's girls had the life of little movie stars, the clothes, the room, the fluff and the stuff a big part of me wanted. I remember Priscilla's canopy bed and her little balcony and that huge, deep tub oh how I loved that tub! These things were the black envy of my every visit; I had to constantly battle my inner grasper whenever I went to Uncle Lloyd's. I like to think I've subdued the grasper now, but I never let my sentinel sleep at her post.

I always wondered if Uncle Lloyd's girls knew how lucky they were. Did they understand their lives were very different from mine? Did they spend as much time feeling lucky as they did griping about having to practice piano? I never did get around to asking.

Those few magical moments in the farmhouse in Brookfield were the anchor I clung to for survival years after we'd moved on. That place is the reason I moved back to New Hampshire. The memories of being surrounded by so many cousins, brought me back. It was a life in which, for thirty seconds I was actually able to be a child, to run, to hike, to sleep over at Uncle Currie's, share secrets with Linda, drool over my cousin Currie's ability to carve anything he saw, follow Noni around like a puppy and where I developed a school girl crush on Paul. Although he nearly suffocated me in a game of hide-and-seek once when he locked me in the cupboard of a big desk I'd decided to hide in my affection for him never wavered.

There, in Brookfield, I had a chance to play with my "twin" cousin, Richard, who was born on the same day, the same year I was. We were inseparable, though I was always a little ticked that he could spell California before I could and I was born there.

Somehow that didn't seem fair to me. His spelling ability also meant he was always the teacher when we played school together. I'm not certain my pride has fully recovered from that.

In those woods behind the farmhouse, I read till I was dizzy, of places I might never see. That house, that tiny spot of ground in one of the tiniest states in the Union, was my childhood, my refuge, and my cousins made it sweeter than it probably was.

My cousins have served as a bridge from the realities of my life to the images of what is possible. They are one of the reasons I have an ounce of sanity left. They were a step away from siblings but closer in many ways than siblings ever get. That small distance gave me the freedom to voice opinions my folks did not always want to hear. Though they were not my siblings, they were still family, raised by parents who still held to the edict issued for millennia, "Have fun but don't talk about family."

Now that we've lost Uncle Cal, the last of my father's siblings, we cousins have become the upper limbs of our family tree. I hope we can open up our scrapbooks and see more clearly what we've all been up to for the past sixty or seventy years, and I think it's time we "talked about family."

Note: *My editor advised me not to give advice.*

As a result I purged these pages of any semblance of advice I could find. I erased bossiness or behavioral modification suggestions I found. I have wiped clean all indications that my way might be your way. But I have chosen to include the following lines, not only because they are important, but also because they have saved me from mind-numbing stress more times than I can list.

So, though I lean on my editor's experience in a field I know little about, I also know there's a lot riding on what people find on these pages. I am including this section as it was first penned and I leave it to my readers to make their own decisions about its usefulness to them.

THE POWER OF NO

Two-year-old children know what adults have long forgotten. No is the most powerful word in the English language. It is also one of the most useful. Life is too short to say yes all the time and, although, if the Doctor told your grandmother she wouldn't live to see seventy-five and she's planned a grand "In your face, Doc" celebration for her hundredth birthday party, serious choices have to be made.

If you're meant to work that day but you haven't gotten the boss' ok for the day off and he insists that you punch in and you haven't been able to twist the arms of any co-workers, brace yourself. My advice is, even though the boss may demand your key to the executive washroom and tell you to pick up your severance pay on your way out the door, "No, I'm sorry, but I can't work that day," is the only answer you can give him. You can find another job, but Gramma's already pushing the envelope, and I say her party gets my vote every time.

Fortunately, most questions requiring a yes or no answer are not as drastic as all that. On the other hand, saying yes every time someone asks something of you, robs you of time to do the things on your own list. If you don't train yourself to say no more often, you'll soon be totally out of time for opportunities that come around once in a lifetime. The problem is, we don't always realize they are once in a lifetime until they've passed us by while we were busy doing something else, for someone else.

You could pick your poison from this list of less than graceful declinations :

- "You must be kidding!"

- "Ain't gonna happen!"

- "Let me count the ways!"

- "You want it when?"

- "You can't be serious!"

- "Don't even ask!"

- "You haven't got a snail's chance in the desert of getting me to do that."

- "Yeah, right!"

- "The last guy who asked me is buried in the basement."

- "I don't think so."

- "Who sicced you on me?"

- "Nyet, nein, no chance!"

- "Don't hold your breath!"

- "Never on Sunday, or any other day!"

On the other hand you could teach yourself to gracefully decline :

- "I know you needed my help last year, but I'm sure you will do fine this year without me I've taught you all I know."

- "You don't really need me for that I've seen you in action; you're a dynamo."

- "Oh, you should ask Mrs. Lennox. She told me she'd love to help with the bake sale."

- "I'd just be in the way."

- "I would have been happy to drive you to the store, but I already made plans for this afternoon."

You could also fall back on:

- "I'm really too busy right now."

- "I'm sorry, I can't this time."

- "I would if I could but I can't."

- Or simply "I just don't want to."

Then, of course, there's always the old standby: "What part of no don't you understand?"

You can try to pass the buck. When I was young, I always put the ball in Dad's court. It was handy to be able to say, "My dad won't allow it." Now that I'm older, I could change it to "If Dad were around, he wouldn't allow me to do that." I'm not sure it would carry the same weight his authority did when I was young, but if I get really desperate, anything's worth a try.

Finding an inoffensive way to answer in the negative can strain one's creativity. The freedom, not to mention the free time it gives you, is worth the strain. Go ahead, strain yourself.

My girlfriend Harriet told me that when she turned eighty she finally declared her independence and learned to say no, without apology or explanation, just a simple "Don't count on me this time." She said it made her drunk with power. Harriet was fifty years my senior, she warned me not to wait so long myself.

There may be only fifty ways to leave your lover, but there are countless ways to just say no.

BE GRATEFUL

Celebrities of every ilk espouse the benefits of keeping a gratitude journal. I can see the importance of such a journal; human beings make lists of import all the time. We have lists with reminders of dates, birthdays, anniversaries, even the dates our bills must be posted. We jot down daily to-do lists so as not to forget what needs attending to. We buy cute address books to keep track of those people we know and love, or those we know we need, a place to record their names, addresses, and phone numbers.

Though some of us still use our Rolodex or have moved into the electronic age and use our computers or our cell phones for keeping those lists, we all have a way of finding people we care about whenever we want to reach out to them.

Science has shown that expressing gratitude, verbally or in writing, privately or with someone else, releases the happiness-inducing hormones oxytocin and dopamine. Gratitude boosts our immune system and quells stress.

Even in private, listing the good qualities of a mate or family members and friends makes you happier because it helps you to see how lucky you are. You don't have to have an audience for gratitude to affect you.

Though many of the folks in our national spotlight see gratitude as not only positive but necessary, it is the ordinary Joe who copes with the traps and snares that come with *not* being at the top of the Forbes 500 list who is in the center of my radar screen.

How does that guy get through the sludge of an increase in his property taxes on Tuesday, the loss of his job on Wednesday, and the week's final humiliation: Thursday's letter from his insurance company informing him that they will not be renewing his homeowner's policy. The reasons being that his home is vacant and uninhabitable. Funny, because he was living there when he closed the door and left for work that morning.

How does he find a reason to be grateful?

His week could be totally ruined by the feeling that he's walking around with a giant target painted on his back, that trouble seeks him out because of it, or he can kindle a fire in the woodstove of his "uninhabitable" house and prepare to do battle with his insurance carrier.

Sometimes the best way to deal with the hideous

misfortunes of not being the richest person on the planet is to come up with a plan. The human brain copes with anything that comes its way if we devise a way to focus.

The ordinary Joe needs to remember that Imperial Ajax Insurance Company, Inc. is not the only game in town, and just because their inspector wouldn't live in his house doesn't mean it can't be home to him.

As I see it, if the ordinary Joe is grateful for the warmth of his fire, a place to hang his hat, and a reason to formulate a plan of action, he's way ahead of anything that may be chasing him. And if he can see the week's craziness as just something that is what it is, he'll beat it every time.

THE POWER OF ROMANCE

Nothing settles a rocking boat or secures its moorings faster than romance. Romance is a lot like sex, really, or books or movies or food: everyone's view of it is unique.

I knew a woman who thought an occasional foot massage was the most romantic gift her husband ever gave her. For me, you wouldn't want to go there; nobody touches my feet without risking serious injury.

One of my favorite romantic gestures is when Hank rises early to start a fire and bring me a cup of coffee before my eyes are fully open. The twenty minutes sprawled out in our bed in anticipation of the coffee, whose aroma wafts up and coaxes me into semi consciousness, is my definition of true romance.

I know this leaves you cold if you're a morning person who pops out of bed like bread from a toaster, but this only further supports my point: One person's idea of romance is anathema to the next. And don't worry, there are support groups for all you early risers. It's a minor affliction, and with the right help and encouragement it can be overcome.

My husband is one of the most romantic men on the planet to me. Many of the romantic gestures he makes don't fit the Hollywood stereotype. They wouldn't even make the cut of trailers for the so-called romantic movies spewed out for summer release, but they melt my butter every single time.

Surprise picnics, perfectly timed, have soothed my battered mind and beaten body so many times I can't even count them. One in particular jumps up and down for my attention. About fifteen years ago I was working a very long day for a boss with a very short fuse. Not only was he abusive but he was also unaware of the skill and loyalty of his crew. On top of that, he had no people skills whatsoever. The words thank you and I'm sorry never graced his lips. He had zero charisma.

One night I had flown home on a late flight from Seattle, missed my connection in Chicago and landed in Manchester three hours from work at two o'clock in the morning. By the time I gathered my luggage and hit the road it was nearly three, and I still managed to punch in at six. We had a deadline to meet, and I had told the boss I'd be back to work that morning.

I hadn't had any sleep, the boss was under pressure and behaving badly, targeting the whole crew but seemingly focusing special attention on me. At the lunch break I called Hank to whine about being taken for granted and feeling generally unappreciated and to tell him when I would be off so he'd know when to pick me up.

On our way home Hank pulled the truck off the road and backed up to the lily pond. After dropping the tailgate he spread out an impromptu picnic. Tough not to love a guy with those kinds of tricks up his sleeve.

Hank is still sweeping me off my feet. Yesterday I was at work an hour and a half longer than I'd planned and when I came through the door he had a fire going in the woodstove, the coffee was primed for brewing, and my tub was filled and steaming, awaiting my tired frame. Whoever says romance is dead never met a guy like Hank.

When it comes to romance or sex my father gave me the best advice I've ever heard on the subject. He told me that when Hank and I were together, if each of us was happy and fulfilled when we emerged to face the world again, we would be experts. He said that no matter what the books or the movies espoused and tried to convince us everyone agreed with, the only opinions that mattered were our own.

As I see it, the real trick is to separate your idea of

romance from anyone else's definition of it. And you just have to trust your own ability to recognize romance when it puts the coffee on.

THE SPARKLERS

THAT LIGHT LIFE'S DARKENED HALLWAYS

Sparklers are, for me, those moments I cannot conjure up without being transported to a happier time and place. They light up any time I need them enough to reach into my past and revisit them.

I am often struck by the power of the written word. Though I've heard all the platitudes about it since I was first able to string words together and weave a sentence, I am still struck by the power of words to unwind my clock.

I have been looking through some old notebooks and journals, trying to pinpoint how I've navigated some of the storms life has put in my path. Some of those notebooks contained references to the ordinary events of my ordinary days; in others I found stories of incidents, seemingly unimportant at the time, that not only made that ordinary life sparkle but also created an emotional reserve I still rely on for support.

When I was nine years old, I went to New York City with my dad. He was on a buying trip, purchasing fabrics needed for his next project and new dreams, and I was lucky enough to go along. While we were in the city, we went to the Waldorf Astoria. We didn't *stay* there, we just *went* there.

When we stepped into the lobby, Dad said, "Take a good look around and enjoy it as much as you can. You may never get back here again."

With that he left me to run to the men's room, telling me he would be right back. I sat down at one of the beautiful desks, pulled a sheet of paper from the drawer, and was in the middle of writing a letter to Gramma when I heard someone calling my name. A bellhop was repeating "Message for Peggy DeBow." When the initial shock passed, I waved him over and told him I was Peggy DeBow. He handed me an envelope and inside, in my father's handwriting, was a note that simply said, "Guess who loves you." After so many hurried midnight embarkations, I no longer have the note, but I can tell you I have read it over in my head hundreds of times, often when Dad and I were in the midst of a standoff. Many times the memory of it has kept me from total despair.

Recently I was sorting through other bits and boxes, of which I have way too many, and I found a battered light blue spiral notebook. I often jot things down in these notebooks and promptly forget where I put them, so that usually when I desperately need a place to write something of import down I can't find a notebook.

I had been working for quite a while so I sat back, cracked the notebook open and began to read. Before I had finished, I'd had a good cry and spent an hour on a beach three thousand miles away from here. This piece was written at Harris Beach, on the Oregon

Coast on September 5, 1980.

The church party is today, so we brought the trailer over last night. We are at Harris Beach. Right now I am sitting in the car watching the sea and the kids playing in the sand below me. Everything is so beautiful here and the smell is fantastic.

Huge gray gulls have gathered around the car now; a man one space over has been throwing bread out for them. They are so graceful in the air and so funny on the ground. They huddle together in little bunches, peeping and screeching at one another, fighting over bits of bread. Now and then a scrawny white one joins them, always looking rather lost.

They scrunch their cheeks down into their chests and raise their shoulders, if seagulls have shoulders, to protect their little bodies from this piercing wind. When someone walks up the sidewalk, they turn and, one by one, catch the updraft and glide out toward the sea.

Hank has just gone over to where the kids are and he's helping them build a sandcastle. This time we remembered to bring all the Jello molds, shovels, egg boxes, and bowls we could shove into a bag. It should turn into quite a castle. From up here they all look like kids, and I guess they really are Hank was smart enough not to "grow up" like everyone else. If I'm lucky, he'll be thirteen for as long as he lives.

I have so much work to do, I should be crocheting, but every time I pick up my hook I think of something else I should write down. There really isn't anything about this trip that's unique, except Bethany found a ten dollar bill on the beach. We've done it all before, often, and I suppose we'll do it many more times, but one day when I'm cleaning out a trunk and tossing things I had no business keeping, I'll find it. I'll look at the date and quickly estimate how old the kids must have been, then I'll read it, and even if I'm in the middle of a desert, I'll be at Harris Beach with Hank and the kids again.

I'll look up and watch the kites hit an air pocket and drop ten feet, catch a breeze and soar again. I'll hear the constant, unhurried sound of surf polishing shore, breathe in that invigorating smell of all these good beach things I'll see Hank and the kids hauling water from the stream to their castle and I'll be here - no matter where I am, I'll be here.

Some of the sparklers in my life are so simple, so ordinary, most people would miss them entirely. But for me they are the things that keep me going when many other coping mechanisms have deserted me. They are touchstones, connecting me to my past and anchoring me to the present.

The fact that my father's mother actually took the time to iron my tiny undershirts before she snugged them down over my head and my pale, boney shoulders can give me a warm embrace anytime I need one. It was not a big thing, not even a very important one since we lived in Southern California at the time. It was simply an act of love from a grandmother who may have felt a chill in the air and wanted to protect me. But whenever I recall it, she warms me all over again.

Some of my sparklers came as compliments, nothing huge by "Awards Ceremony Standards," just simple things, a comment on a particular outfit or the hat I'd chosen to wear that day. When my dad, a sign painter extraordinaire, told me my freehand lettering was better than that of my big brother, John, I counted it high praise, indeed. I thought John was an artistic genius.

My brightest sparklers, those that can penetrate any dark cloud, are love letters from Hank. They are so important, so highly valued that I have often made copies of them so that by the time I've reread them a hundred times, I have a backup to hold me up when the darkness closes in.

I made a copy of the last one he wrote before he came home from his most recent trip to the hospital. I knew if I lost him it would be my lifeline later on. I had the printer shrink it for me so I could put it in my key chain and carry it with me wherever I go.

I will miss Hank if he dies before I do but not because I don't know how to write a check, or don't know how much we still owe on the house, or how much the car payment is. We had a different sort of partnership and I would be a different sort of widow. There are so many soft shadows he has cast across my life the emptiness his departure would bring is ethereal, it could not be measured.

Hank has sparklers of his own. He says the reason he came through his last ordeal, those horrible days on life support, was that every time his meds loosened their grip and he fought his way to some lucidity, he scanned the room for two things, me and the wall of photographs I had put up.

I had taped up shots of everything from our wedding day to the kids, even a shot of the cabin we built the first year we lived in New Hampshire. He said they brought him back to the present and that each time he looked up and saw them he knew he was going home. In fact, his main wish the whole time he was in the hospital was to go home and share coffee with me on the porch of that little cabin in our yard. What he wanted most was to sit in the waning days of autumn and drink coffee on that porch.

BIG GIRLS DO CRY

THE SMART ONES DO ANYWAY

This afternoon I was scanning some emails I'd written to my big brother. I was hunting for a letter I'd shared with him, a letter written to our father years after we'd lost him. While searching I found myself reading some of the things I had written, several of them sent while my husband was hospitalized the year before last.

My words took my breath away. I experienced the same visceral reaction I have every time I see a rerun of that first plane hitting one of the twin towers.

Then I cried. Tears I had no time or energy for while Hank was fighting for his life, tears I wasn't able to shed when I should have, hit me like Uncle Fred's line drive that knocked me out when I was nine years old.

For a long time I cried over all my husband had gone through, for the helplessness I felt while he lay there helpless. I shed tears for all we had gone through, and, finally, I cried tears of immeasurable joy over having him home again, over waking to the sound of his breathing and the warmth of his hand when I reach for him in the middle of the night.

But I waited too long. I should have found the time, a place where I felt safe, "me time" to mourn lost moments and quell rising fears. There is no telling what a year of pent up emotion may have done to my body.

Dad said the smartest people on the planet are the ones who learn from their mistakes. Next time I'm faced with pressures like those of the past two years, I'll remind myself that it never hurts to have a good long cry and the sooner, the better.

MORE ABOUT PORCHES

Before I offer my final thoughts, I wanted to squeeze in a few more arguments in favor of porches, you can never have too many reasons for tacking on a porch - just ask Hank.

FIREFLIES

The fireflies of my childhood summers in New Hampshire were so magical to me I thought of little else during the evenings when they were on full display. I could hardly wait for the sun to set. The fireworks of the Fourth of July did not interest me as much as the fireflies. These tiny creatures could light up my summers just by searching for each other in the cool of the evenings. They trumped the fireworks every time: Nobody had to load them and get the timing just right. We didn't have to pile everybody into the car in the heat just to drive somewhere else to see them and Dad didn't have to referee until the winners of the shotgun or window seats had been decided; we simply sat on the porch and waited for the show to commence.

SUMMER SLEEP-OVERS

No other spot on the lake, in the mountains, or at the beach is as perfect for a sleepover as a porch. A screen is nice if the mosquitoes are the size of hummingbirds but a screen is not necessary. Sleeping on the porch keeps you connected to family but far enough away to share secrets with your cousins and steal out of bed in the early hours to enjoy the intoxicating scents that disappear when the barometer changes as the sun comes up.

STORM WATCHING

It has been said that the best things in life are free, and nothing proves that better than sitting, feet propped up on the rail, windblown and damp from stray raindrops, watching the fury of a thunderstorm play itself out against the background of the mountains or the sea. In fact, watching a storm gather strength and speed then pour into the valley at Mount Moosilauke's feet is awe-inspiring and more entertaining than going to the movies.

Snowfall becomes a living thing as it winds its way down the mountainside and into the valley. If you're watching the snow fall from your porch you need a mug of something warm to hang on to; not only will it keep your hands comfortable, but it will encourage you to linger until the wind has blown snowflakes up under the eaves and onto your lap. In New Hampshire nothing is as satisfying as a perfectly brewed cup of coffee fogging your glasses while you watch the birth of a blizzard from your porch.

A GREAT PLACE FOR A BREAK

If I am faced with a deadline, I often push myself to work nonstop for hours at a time. Fortunately for me, Hank will coax me away from my work long enough to share a cup of coffee on the porch. He knows I get so engrossed in whatever project I'm working on that I will go all day without leaving my workbench. He also knows a fresh cup of coffee in my favorite earthenware mug is irresistible to me, and a few moments on the porch with my feet against the railing is all the break I need. After that no deadline is unreachable.

A NON-PORCH PORCH WILL DO IN A PINCH

Anyplace will serve as a porch if you are part of the sad majority in this country who do not have one.

A blanket on the lawn will serve, the nearest library will do in less than perfect weather, even the laundromat could double as a porch, and if you have a load to wash, you can multitask. The nice things about turning the laundromat into a porch are, that the lighting is excellent, you can count on it being warm, and there are always tables if you want a place to put your coffee or a basket of yarn.

I have one friend who lives forty-five minutes from one side of town and another who lives forty-five minutes in the opposite direction I meet the first one at Burger King; we refer to it as HQ. And I meet the other in the upstairs lounge of a local senior center after her art class. We live far apart and, though we all have porches from adequate to wow, amazing we create a porch for ourselves anytime we want to get together far from our homes.

The most important thing about a porch is not its size or its view but the comfort and camaraderie it inspires, the opportunity it provides for us to stay connected to the people in our lives who matter most and to make connections with those people who might become part of that group.

MY NEUTRAL ZONE

When discussions become too intense, tempers flare, or problems are allowed to be blown out of all reasonable proportions, I retreat to the porch. The sanctuary it provides makes it possible to gather my wits and reassess the issue at hand.

My porch gives me separation from a problem's immediacy; it offers a space in which to take a cleansing breath and see the real size and import of anything I have to face. Out there I can temporarily retreat without actually running away.

INTICING AND INVITING

On my way to work I pass a house at Four Corners. It is empty during the winter, but lately I have noticed a lady sitting in the afternoon shade of her porch, her knitting in her lap. When I take the bend I have to force myself onward because seeing her sitting there is an invitation to me, one I can barely resist. Every time I see her out there I want to pull into her driveway just to stop and introduce myself and to see what she's been knitting. One day soon I intend to.

WORRY FREE ZONE

My home is the only place in the universe where I have complete privacy and freedom. People don't get a guided tour of the rooms just because they chanced to come by while I was at home. On my porch I can entertain or just converse with nothing more expected of me. Out there I don't have to explain the clutter or excuse my perceived negligence. My porch is a miniature demilitarized zone, the boundaries set to include as many passing friends as it will hold.

And in case you haven't figured it out yet, I love porches.

IT IS WHAT IT IS

Life is full of *stuff* that just happens some we can fix, some things we can't. The trick is to cultivate an attitude of "It is what it is." The honest truth is, that much of what happens to us simply happens, often with no contribution on our part. We don't start much of it, and there's very little of it we can actually stop from happening. The only important thing is how we handle what happens to us, what we do about what's already been done.

If your gas gauge is on the fritz and you run out of gas on the way to an important meeting, how it happened is far less important than how you handle it.

If you lose control and cuss out the faulty gauge, the idiot mechanic who didn't catch it when he did the last inspection, the manufacturer who built that piece of junk, the misguided designer who drew up the plans, the little jerk who sold it to you and the fact that you never had the money to afford a decent car your problem still exists, you're still out of gas, still late for your meeting and while you've wasted so much time fuming about it absolutely nothing has changed except your blood pressure and your mental state.

So many of us grew up watching Sesame Street, we behave as though we believe life is lived in thirty-second increments, that all problems should resolve themselves before the Count starts counting or Cookie Monster raids the next cookie jar. Most of us want the *stuff* that happens to go away, quicker than it came, preferably. Unfortunately, real life is a bit more complicated, and no matter how cute the singing artichoke is he can't just hum a happy tune and fix everything.

"It is what it is" can be a valuable mantra. Repeating it loud and often will do more for your well-being than finding someone to blame for faulty gauges, empty tanks, missed appointments, or any other *stuff* that happens.

Repeat after me: "It is what it is."

I NEED TO SAY IT NOW

Recently I took a moment to flip through the photo album in my head, to picture the people who've been there for me through the storms of life, the folks who taught me things I might never have learned if I'd never met them. I decided to close my eyes and visit somebody I never thanked or apologized to. There have been so many choosing just one was impossible.

I asked myself how much guilt I would drag around

with me and for how long, if I don't get those things said, those messages sent. For me, now is the time to answer those questions, the time to say the things I've been too busy for or perhaps too embarrassed to address.

How would I feel if I let this moment pass me by?

Now is the time for me to say:

- "I'm glad we met."

- "Thank you for --."

- "You're more important to me than you'll ever know."

- "I envy your ability to--."

- "You are the best cook [gardener etc.] I ever met."

- "Thank you for teaching me --."

- "I'm so sorry about --."

- "I love you." (It is impossible to say this too often.)

Between Gramma's love of flowers and Dad's insistence on a garden wherever we stopped long enough for man or melon to take root, I grew up believing that no matter how much work, no matter the aching knees from the never-ending job of pulling weeds, a garden was worth the time and effort expended.

When we lived on the farm in Brookfield, New Hampshire I used to sit in the sunshine halfway down a row of partially weeded tomatoes and reward myself with what I considered the finest delicacy nature ever provided. Sitting there in the warmth enjoying the juicy flesh of a sun-ripened tomato with the row's weeding half finished and the sun's rays on my back was, as far as I was concerned, summertime perfection.

Weeding tomatoes offered more than just the flavor of what a tomato is supposed to taste like, it gave me lots of exercise, plenty of vitamin D, a break from the rigors of the life I was living at the time and a chance to let my mind flit around with the butterflies and renew itself, sometimes even heal itself.

I never looked at gardening as just work, I saw it as a refuge and it's work as rebirth not of body perhaps, but certainly of soul, I still do. I never thought to thank Dad and Gramma for introducing me to the pleasures of the garden.

I cannot let another day go by in which I say, "I wish I had."

Life is not always fair; it doesn't always color inside the lines.

But remember even the darkest hour is still only sixty minutes long.

TIPS FROM THE MAN ON THE STREET

I asked some people what they do to unwind, how they cope with real life when it gets out of control, and what solace they reach for when they're beaten by life's storms or are battling realities they cannot rein in. These are some of those responses, in their own words.

NYC cabbie : "I have a boat. When I finish my workweek, I hop in my boat head out until I can't see the city anymore, then I drop anchor and let the city sounds melt away. After that, I can face anything."

Waitress : "I set the VCR to record my favorite soap opera. When I get home from work I settle into my favorite chair and watch it. It just lets me unwind. I've been watching it since I was in high school."

Chef : "Pot. And I don't mean one to cook in or one to shove under the bed I mean the one that mellows, that softens the edges of my life. A toke or two and I'm ready to tackle any of life's problems."

Head chef at popular Vermont restaurant: "I take a drive. I go down to my boyhood home in southern New Hampshire, wander around a little, gain a new perspective, my life's not so bad after all."

Construction supervisor : "When I get home the first thing I do is grab a shower to wash away my day.

Then I find a comfortable place to sit down with my wife and discuss our plans and goals. It's the refresher that keeps me on track."

Homemaker : "No matter how stressful the issue, I remind myself that it is just a moment, one moment that will soon become a distant memory."

My prince : "I try to find another way to view problems or problem people. Bitterness keeps others at a distance, and, in the end, bitter people find themselves alone. If you can drum up a little pity for them, annoyance melts away."

Recurring themes with everybody : humor, music, teddy bears and cats or other pets. And those of You who don't like cats - I think we need to talk.

Maggie Anderson lives in the White Mountains of New Hampshire with her husband Hank and a self-absorbed black cat named Cry Baby.

When the author isn't braving New Hampshire's frigid winters, providing transfusions for the black flies or fighting off mosquitoes the size of humming birds, she spends much of her time trying to keep her teddy bear, Ethan From, out of harm's way

Made in the USA
Middletown, DE
23 October 2023

41137265R00073